ROCK SOLID
Relationship

**Seven Keys to Restore Your Connection
& Make Your Love Last**

Norene Gonsiewski, MSW, LCSW
Timothy Higdon, MS, LPC

LASTING LOVE PRESS
Portland, Oregon

Editor / Ruth Matinko-Wald
Graphic Design / Susan Luckey Higdon

ISBN 0692415939

For questions or permission requests,
Email imagonorene@gmail.com.

Lasting Love Press
2804 SE 28th Avenue
Portland, Oregon 97202
United States of America

Printed in the United States of America

Dedication

To our Rock Solid spouses,
Tom and Susan.
Without their love and continual support, we would not
have written this book nor would we have Rock Solid Relationships of our own.

To all of the couples who have entrusted us
with your precious relationships:
You have taught us as much as any of the relationship gurus.

And to our coach, Henry Harlow, who has guided us through
every step of getting our message to those who need it.

Preface

Allow us to introduce ourselves! We are dedicated educators, counselors, and coaches in the field of committed relationships. Combined, we have over 65 years of personal experience working with couples. Moreover, we both have spent countless time studying the work of masters in the field. Our school of couples counseling, Imago Relationship Theory, was developed by Harville Hendrix and Helen LaKelly Hunt. Much of the advice you will read in this book comes from their work, which has continued to be enriched by others such as Maya Kollman, Master Trainer in Imago Therapy.

In addition to our Imago-informed views on what creates and maintains rock solid relationships, we refer to the work of many other teachers. Gary Chapman, Bill Doherty, Mort Fertel, Helen Fisher, Shirley Glass, John Gottman, Susan Johnson, Pat Love, Pepper Schwartz, Dan Siegel, Janis Abrahms Spring, and Stan Tatkin are just a few of the theorists who have added invaluable research, wisdom, and tools to the field of marriage counseling.

We also wish to acknowledge the time and efforts of our editor, Ruth Matinko-Wald and our graphic designer Susan Luckey Higdon. Both women went far beyond our expectations to deliver a product well worth your time to read.

In *Rock Solid Relationship*, we draw upon this wealth of information as well as the thousands of hours we have spent helping couples to repair and enrich their relationships. We are certain the material in this book will help you to be among those couples who spend a lifetime sharing love.

Norene Gonsiewski, MSW, LCSW
imagonorene@gmail.com
503 234-4440

Timothy Higdon, MS, LPC
tth@bendcable.com
541 330-9782 ext. 1

Contents

Introduction

"No masterpiece was ever created by a lazy artist."

—Anon.

Y ou have picked up this book for one of two reasons: You are a proactive person looking for tools to keep your marriage or partnership strong, or, more likely, you are struggling with your marriage or partnership and are desperate for help. If you're the former, good for you! Every page of *Rock Solid Relationship* is filled with valuable information that will fortify your relationship. If you're struggling, chin up! There is hope! Throughout the pages of this short book, we will share with you the seven keys to restore the connection you once enjoyed and to make your love last.

Not married? Our book is still for you. In today's world, marriage is no longer the norm, the gold standard, or the status symbol it once was, and intimate relationships now come in many shapes. In order to be inclusive, we use the terms *relationship, partnership,* and *marriage* interchangeably and deliberately. Whatever type of relationship you have, we have written this book for you, because we know your love can last. You just need to learn the tools to make your relationship so rock solid that it will stand the test of time.

Actually, now may possibly be the best time in modern history to be seeking relationship advice. Because of recent social and scientific research, we have an ever-growing body of useful information about relationships: why certain people are attracted to each other, what makes bonds flourish or fail, the up-and-down predictable stages of relationships, and how certain behaviors trigger certain responses. Through understanding this research—and putting into practice the time-tested advice of relationship experts—you can learn to resolve conflict, bring passion back into your life, and, ultimately, create the rock solid relationship of your dreams.

Build Your Love to Last

In your dreams, do you and your partner both feel warmth, respect, a sense of adventure, and deep affection? That loving connection is possible—even despite the difficulties you are facing or will inevitably face. We know so because of our many decades of coaching couples over the hurdles of conflict. The research noted above and our work point to certain behaviors that support resilience in relationships. These behaviors can help couples return their relationship to its "original shape after it has been pulled, stretched, pressed, and bent;" Webster's definition of resilience.

What are those resilience-building behaviors? What makes a relationship hardy, able to weather storms, and spring back from troubles? In a nutshell, resilient relationships are ones in which both partners develop and maintain a "relationship savings account," and our seven keys outline the "currency" of loving kindnesses, appreciations, sexual intimacy, affection, protective boundaries, and other caring words and actions to fund that account.

Just like financial bank accounts, relationship savings accounts offer us needed security. When we have enough savings, we can relax and manage the occasional withdrawal. When the savings account is low, though, we become anxious—and a withdrawal could throw us into relational bankruptcy. Knowing this, happy couples continually make an effort to work on their relationship by making "deposits." Over time, they become relaxed and trust their needs can be met and that their love can last. Couples in trouble can triage by working extra hard on making "deposits" to refill an empty account. Eventually, they can build trust and feel confident their love can last, too.

In truth, building any relationship savings account with scheduled deposits and strong growth from compound interest takes effort. The work may not be easy—but it will be worth the energy. The place to start is by figuring out why you stopped making deposits with the regularity you once did during your courtship phase, also known as the infatuation or honeymoon phase. Often the culprit is our unconscious and inaccurate beliefs about the nature of romantic love. Did you think, for example, when you married or committed yourself to Mr. or Ms. "Perfect," that you would just live happily ever after with lots of romance and little conflict? If you did, you shouldn't feel alone. That flawed thinking is based on a persistent cultural myth perpetuated in movies, literature, songs, and sitcoms!

Another cultural phenomenon affecting regular relationship savings account "deposits" is that younger people are committing to their relationships later in life, if at all, and with skepticism. That is, people once married as an expected step in adulthood, a means to move forward in life, the trigger for getting a job, an apartment, a car, etc. Today, however, those that do marry view their partnership more as the capstone to an already established life. Having gotten accustomed to having everything "their way," many newlyweds now expect to be able to have the "self" they know and love remain completely intact when they merge with another. This, of course, is not possible.

No Need to Despair

Whatever the error in thinking about a permanent state of romance, we are all disappointed when the infatuation phase is over. You may avoid the wedding, but you can't avoid the end of the honeymoon. In reality, despite all the romantic feelings in the world, all couples eventually have relationship challenges. The emergence of these challenges is one of the predictable stages of relationships. Because our family and friends never share this fact—and because the media never plays it up—when the challenges continue and perhaps worsen, we feel disappointed, become disillusioned, and finally reach despair. Disappointed and disillusioned, we often let our romantic relationships slide into bad habits. We replace our warm and easy giving and receiving with unpleasant behaviors such as becoming reactive and defensive, ignoring the other's needs, and being lazy about giving gifts and spending time together.

A sadder truth is that, even if our parents or friends had told us to expect a phase of mounting challenges, and to hang in there and work on the relationship, we wouldn't have believed them. Romantic love is designed with high hopes—and blinders! Also, the conflicts of the relationship challenge phase provide opportunities for growth, and growth is often uncomfortable. We all love the honeymoon phase. The second phase, not so much!

Perhaps the greatest challenge to lasting commitment is that we aren't with someone who's just like us. Your partner has his or her own thoughts, feelings, needs, and preferences. No one ever told you that one day you would struggle with this fact, but everyone does. We all want things our way, and we all believe our thoughts and feelings are "right." We think if our partner were more like us, we would fight less and be more passionate.

In fact, couples suffer under the myth that romantic relationships are based on compatibility. This myth says that, if we are with the "right" person, he or she will think, feel, and act as we do. Based on the myth, we unconsciously think our partner should share our views, want to please us all the time, never behave in ways we disapprove, enjoy the same activities, and have the same family traditions and values. Even online dating sites tout compatibility as the key to happiness in relationships. So untrue!

The illusion of a perfect fit is part of the infatuation phase when we are getting help from intoxicating endorphins. In truth, compatibility is a misconception and overrated. Instead of looking for compatibility, we should be striving to become good companions. A companion is a partner whose *qualities and opinions complement*, not necessarily match, your own. The definition of complement is to add to something in a way that enhances or improves it, to make something perfect.

Conflict=An Opportunity to Grow

We need to understand that our areas of incompatibility are not recipes for unhappiness but opportunities to learn how to become a successful companion—whose complementary traits will help us to be a fulfilled person. We can do this through good communication and stretching into giving our partner what he or she really needs.

In our counseling offices, almost daily we hear couples say their unhappiness is because they are *different* from each other—whether because they have divergent hobbies, parenting styles, money views, or family backgrounds. Feeling upset and hopeless about whether you will ever get what you need from your partner is normal, but you didn't pair up with yourself. You fell in love with a person different from you, because opposites really do attract. You were supposed to build a life with someone different from you, and, hopefully, both of you would eventually grow into people who could give and take with ease.

Although hard work, this is an expected and necessary stage in all romantic relationships, because everyone picks partners with important differences. In essence, we aren't fully complete people ourselves, with every facet of our humanity developed perfectly. Even if you waited until your life was established and sought your relationship as a capstone, as many in the Millennial Generation (those born between 1980-2000) do, there are certain skills you cannot master without a partner to push along your growth. For example, by being in a relationship that has some conflict, we push the buttons left over from childhood and finally deal with our "baggage." And, being with someone who has different traits gives us a chance to improve ourselves and to grow new interests and skills. How does that growth happen? It happens when we accept the challenge to learn how to engage in conflict in a manner that doesn't leave either of us feeling wrong or less than equal. When you master this skill, you and your partner will finally feel like real teammates. You will both bloom into your full potential. Aren't those things we all strive for?

As a matter of fact, once couples hit the phase of relationship challenges, most will require some form of counseling, coaching, or relationship education in order to build or rebuild a rock solid connection. All enduring, intimate connections require safety and tools that couples can use to sort out the inevitable disagreements in a way that feels healthy and fair. Unfortunately, most couples wait six or more years to get the help they need! By the time they go to counseling, take a marriage education workshop, or work together through a self-help book, they are already in despair with one or both partners contemplating leaving the relationship. The hallmark phrase of this state of despair is, "I love my partner, but I'm not in love any more."

But breaking up is NOT the only solution! Don't be the lazy artists who hope to dabble until they have a masterpiece. Be the artists who work diligently, lovingly revisiting the canvas day-by-day and year-by-year until the technique is truly masterful. This book can help you! It's a manual of what to do to make your relationship rock solid. No matter how bad your relationship has become, once you begin to make small changes, you will be surprised at how rapidly you develop the habits that make you—and your partner—feel loved again.

You can do this—with some effort and genuine, generous love!

Finding Love and Losing It

"You know you're in love when you don't want to fall asleep because reality is finally better than your dreams."

—Dr. Suess

Remember new love? Butterflies in the stomach, hugging and kissing, gift-giving, fun dates and adventures, hours spent talking into the night, sharing of dreams and desires, maybe even amazing sex. This first stage of romantic relationships, called "infatuation" or "courtship" or "honeymoon", is the time of attraction and attachment. During this phase, Mother Nature gives us the gift of regular doses of endorphins, the hormones that make us feel in love, attached, and hopeful. We emphasize "feel," because the hormones of romance trigger feelings that spark us to be our best, most incredible selves and to see only the best qualities in our new lover. When we are high on these hormones—and they do make us high—we act in ways that show each other how much love we feel. In other words, we make "deposits" in our "relationship savings account."

New love is never boring or lazy. It is characterized by high energy, increased sexual desire, and tireless efforts to win the love and commitment of the other person who we come to feel is our soul mate. The infatuation chemicals also build in us a "tunnel vision" about what makes our partner happy, and they make us so "high" we honestly believe we could paint a masterpiece effortlessly!

The wonderful emotional highs and consistent positive, passionate interactions during this infatuation phase of relationships are actually designed to bond people to one another. Think about our cavemen ancestors. A lot of adversity existed during those ancient times, so our attachment needed to be strong enough to overcome all the obstacles of pair bonding so as to ensure the continuation of the species.

How did the infatuation stage look in your early relationship? Think back. You have a unique love story about how you met and became infatuated with each other. You reveled in the "magic power" triggered by the release of endorphins and felt uninhibited and free. The hormones of infatuation reduced your self-consciousness, increased your comfort with closeness, and made you tolerant of your partner's imperfections—if you noticed them at all. You weren't irritated with small things, and you felt magnanimous in your ability to give to your partner. You thought about each other constantly, and, when you weren't together, you wondered what the other was doing. Even if you stayed up all night talking, you still bounced up the next morning for work. You effortlessly and automatically made your partner the biggest priority in your life.

What Happened to the Magic?

Fast forward to now. Do you still prioritize your relationship? If the answer is no, what happened? For starters, you made a commitment and moved in together. That began the shift from what each of you imagined your life together would be like to the reality of how it actually is—filled with demanding job deadlines, exhausting nights up with sick children, mandatory Sunday evening dinners with the in-laws, never-ending house repairs, and more.

On top of everyday demands, the "honeymoon" hormones didn't kick in anymore. Over time, infatuation hormones fade for everyone; it's a natural evolutionary process. After a certain period of time, the brain decides the pair bonding occurred and the extra chemicals aren't needed anymore. The reason this happens is because, in the time of our ancestors, a child would have been conceived and the couple would have settled into ensuring the child's—and species'—survival.

At this stage, an inevitable "relationship challenge phase" commences. Without the extra endorphins on board to keep us focused on our partner, we attempt to multi-task. Children and other competing forces vie for priority, which may cause anxiety. And some of us just get lazy. As the "feel good" hormones of romantic love wane and the tiring tasks of real life set in, we retreat to the path of least resistance—basically plopping down and doing what is the easiest.

Think about what happens when we get a new car. For a while, we keep it perfectly clean and free of clutter, but, over time, we begin to eat in the car, leave a little trash, and even forget to take out the dirty gym socks. Although we didn't stop needing our car and benefiting from it, we stopped making its maintenance our priority. We do the same in romantic relationships! We slip into bad habits instead of turning the *good behaviors* Mother Nature triggered us to do automatically during the infatuation stage into *good habits*. We stop making the daily deposits of love and passion in the "relationship savings account," start fighting or retreating, and begin to feel as though our once-beloved soul mate is now our cell mate.

In essence, in your relationship, as the infatuation phase naturally waned, you both lost your "magic powers" to make the other feel like a million bucks. You also lost your tolerance for all those small imperfections and started to see your partner's flaws in Technicolor. In fact, you picked up a magnifying glass and exaggerated your partner's shortcomings! You probably did not examine your own diminished treatment of your partner, because humans always pay more attention to how someone is hurting them rather than examing their own behavior.

In addition to the very common behaviors above, childhood wounds or hurt from past relationships might have surfaced for you or your partner after the "blinders" of the infatuation stage came off. Past wounds and hurt easily can get in the way of closeness and connection, because we all decode our partner's messages largely based on our previous experiences.

Over time, all the conflicts made you feel discouraged and despondent about your relationship. You might have tried to get the "magic powers" back, but you couldn't. Feeling hurt, you disconnected and stopped prioritizing your relationship. When you stopped prioritizing your relationship, you stopped contributing all the necessary ingredients for lasting love: patience, tolerance, acceptance, affection, compassion, interest, affirmation, playfulness, sexual prowess, and humor. You eventually began to associate time spent with your partner with disappointment and pain. This association became so strong that it wired your brain to automatically view your partner and your marriage with negativity and even disdain.

The Slippery Slope

All couples have their own versions of distraction and the slippery slope into disconnection and ultimately an atmosphere of distance. No relationship turns out exactly as we hope! In reality, other life commitments always make relationships less than what we imagine. But, when the relationship becomes an afterthought and is put on the backburner, tension and stress arises. The disconnection can cause a slippery slope to conflict and lead to resentment, disappointment, and discouragement. You become less and less available and present with one another. Instead of talking out a conflict, you act it out. You come home and plop down in front of a screen and barely say "hi" to your partner. You find more and more that needs to get done at work. You want your girls' or guys' night out, instead of date night with your honey. You spend hours on Facebook instead of talking and cuddling. The kids' needs are more important than your relationship needs. Think of these as *avoidance* behaviors. You are consciously or unconsciously avoiding the conflict you are convinced will arise, while, in the meantime, you are creating good reasons for future upsets!

As disconnection increases, partners unconsciously retreat to other activities. We really aren't trying to avoid our partner; in fact, we miss the closeness we once had. Instead, we are trying to avoid the hurt and disappointment.

Typically, we start with smaller avoidance behaviors in which anything can be used to sidestep contact. Examples include work, children, hobbies, friends, TV, emails, gaming, and screen time. They can grow into bigger avoidance behaviors when a pattern persists that significantly damages the relationship. Addictions, affairs, and violence are examples of major breaches of intimacy. They cause you to lose the ability to be vulnerable with each other.

If you are experiencing such a major breach, you will need to seek professional help to change course and create the safety you need to restore your connection. This will require focused work. You will need to learn how to love your partner again. When you make the decision to do this and follow it with actions and behaviors that meet your partner's needs, that's when you will find real love. And when you experience real love, you will make your relationship rock solid.

Reflection

Take a few minutes to write about your personal, unique love story. Where did you meet? What was your new love like? How did it feel? What kind of things did you like to do together?

When did you start to notice the relationship challenge phase? How did each of you react to this stage?

Did you try to get the "magic" back? With what efforts?

How do you and your partner interact now? How much time do you spend together? What distractions keep you apart? Describe how you engage in avoidance behaviors. Put down the magnifying glass and look in the mirror. Be certain not to list your partner's unhelpful behaviors. Look at your own.

What would you like your "happily ever after" to look like?

Looking at the list of your avoidance behaviors, what do you see you could start doing differently right now, in order to achieve your "happily-ever-after" picture?

Key #1

Return Your Partner to Priority Status

"You have to decide what your highest priorities are and have the courage—pleasantly, smilingly, nonapologetically, to say 'no' to other things. And the way you do that is by having a bigger 'yes' burning inside."

—Stephen R. Covey

The bottom line is, if you want lasting love in your life, you will have to make your partner your highest priority. At this stage, doing so might seem daunting. We live in an age when an individual's whims, wishes, and wants too often take precedence over his or her committed relationship. You may not even know what it truly means to put your relationship and your partner first. Or you might not have any clue as to how to do so in the face of careers, children, friends, hobbies, and personal needs. Viewed this way, putting your partner and your relationship first may even sound like a chore.

To return your partner to priority status will require a *focused, conscious effort* on your part. You can't command the unconscious processes that drove you to prioritize your relationship during the romantic, infatuation phase to return, so the effort is up to you—not Nature—now.

How do you make this "conscious" effort? It's a two-step process: 1) Set the intention of raising your relationship's importance to the top, and 2) Initiate daily loving behaviors. That is, to remain greatly in love, you need to *consciously act in ways that show your love.* This means engaging in actions toward each other that "make deposits" into your "relationship savings account."

The number one benefit of making your partner the priority in your life is that your relationship will last—and so will you! Couples who prioritize their relationship feel safe, remain connected, and keep passion alive—all of which contribute to longevity.

Focusing on your relationship brings other benefits as well. Specifically, children thrive when their parents love and support each other; witnessing the commitment and love of parents provides the foundation for a child's self-love and the model of his or her own future romantic relationships. A strong, healthy parental relationship also translates into a sense of security for a child that acts as a protective factor when it comes to risky behaviors such as experimenting with drugs and alcohol. In fact, over 30 years of research continues to reveal how devastating divorce is on children and the legacy it leaves behind (Wallerstein 2004; Emery, 2006; Root, 2010).

Interestingly, prioritizing your relationship also can improve your financial life. Couples who spend more time together are closer and more honest with one another (Eaker Weil, 2010). They don't keep money matters secret to avoid conflict or guilt nor make regrettable spending choices to fill an empty void.

You also will have more fun when you make your partner the priority in your life. In fact, you may trick your brain into thinking you are dating again and have a resurgence of those wonderful "new love" hormones! Imagine how nice it would feel to go to bed at the same time and cuddle, talk, or make love. Imagine how it would feel to see your partner turn off the computer or the television and suggest a walk or a check-in about the day. Do you think it would make you and your partner feel special and loved if you spent less time on self-pursuits and more on couple time? Do you think you might argue less and play more? We know the answer is yes.

Time: A Major "Relationship Savings" Account Deposit

One way you can return your partner to priority status is by spending more time with him or her. Unfortunately, a popular relationship myth claims that, to be happy in a relationship, you need to be happy with your-self first—and that requires spending a lot of time doing things alone or with friends and family other than your partner. Our experience tells us the opposite is true: Instead, happy couples make for happy individuals!

Abandoning some of your personal pursuits and interests early in your relationship happened normally. At one point, you wanted to spend as much time as possible with your love interest, so maybe you stopped play-ing on a basketball league or going out for a drink with friends. Your in-teractions with and actions toward your partner created excitement and enlivened you. In fact, your relationship broadened your horizons, and you discovered new things about yourself because of the other person. In other words, your relationship, especially *your* contribution to the rela-tionship, fulfilled you and made you a better person.

What happened since that early stage of your relationship? Do you now feel you gave up too much for the sake of the relationship and need to recover your sense of self? Have children usurped the number one prior-ity position in your life? Perhaps you didn't stop important involvements but, nonetheless, have begun to feel you contribute more than your part-ner to the relationship. Maybe you have become so discouraged you don't believe you will ever be happy together again, so now you want to return to what once made you happy alone.

Actually, forming resentments and relating to your partner from a self-cen-tered place of "what's in it for me" are quite common and predictable be-haviors in the relationship challenge phase. But there are ways around the conflict—and being in a healthy relationship can truly support each part-ner to get his or her own needs met, without jeopardizing the relationship.

For example, look at Jenny and Jake's situation. Early in their marriage, Jake began playing golf more and more often. He and Jenny had only one day off together. Needless to say, Jenny was none too pleased when Jake filled their free day with tee times. When Jake recognized his partner's dis-appointment and realized that having too little couple time wasn't good for their marriage, he decided to keep their day off sacred. He talked to Jenny about getting outside for a shared relaxing activity, and she agreed.

Once they claimed a consistent time for togetherness, Jake found that Jenny was much more encouraging of his playing golf—and their relationship strengthened.

The truth is, people actually take better care of themselves physically, emotionally, and socially when they have someone to love; a good relationship motivates each partner. We know this because research shows that couples in happy relationships are healthier, feel more fulfilled, and live longer than people living alone or in unhappy relationships. Health studies done by major universities around the world call this "The Marriage Effect," referring to the notable impact that committed relationships have on an individual's health and longevity (Harvard Health Publications, 2010; Parker-Pope, 2010; Proulx, 2013).

The Challenges of Prioritizing Your Partner

It's not hard to imagine why prioritizing another doesn't come easily. Thinking of your partner's needs when yours go unfulfilled can feel like a sacrifice. For example, in the evening, you might want to read a book or call a friend instead of listening to your partner talk about his or her day. The push-pull of your needs versus those of your partner never ceases.

In the past, the prioritization of marriages by couples was the social norm. In general, strong gender roles actually made marriages more romantic, because partners tried to play their part to be a good wife or husband. Just 40 years ago, for example, the average woman prioritized her life thus: husband first, children second, and herself (and possibly her job) third. The average man prioritized his life in the following order: making a living first, his wife second, and his children third.

Over time, however, our society has moved from an emphasis on valuing intimate commitment to valuing consumerism, entertainment, and socializing. Now, both genders prioritize themselves first, children second, and partner third. Switching priorities means having to give up something, and relinquishing some of our autonomy can be quite a challenge.

But here's the thing: The idea of sacrificing for your marriage is an illusion. You *are* half of your marriage, and you benefit when your relationship benefits. Your relationship is the foundation upon which the rest of your life is built, so it always needs to come first. When your marriage is happy, everything else in your life is better.

If you have a pattern of avoidance or poor relating habits that have built up over years, modifying your behavior even a little may seem difficult and finding time for each other may seem impossible. Even turning the TV off and talking to each other a few nights a week may seem strained. What do you talk about? We suggest you start by picking a topic of interest to you both. Or consider preparing a meal together and catching up on the news of your day. A quiet walk in the evening also can do wonders for a relationship that has felt distant.

Reflection

Make a list of the activities that prevent you from making your relationship the priority. Some may be normal parts of life such as making a living, raising children, watching TV, answering emails, exercising or, yes, playing golf.

Which behaviors you are willing to modify or stop in order to put more energy back into your relationship? Coming home earlier from work, getting the kids to bed earlier, playing one less round of golf, leaving the emails until morning, or turning off the TV one or two nights a week are all good examples. Choosing to take any of these small steps and stick with them over time can add up to big changes in your partnership. Before long, the gap between you will close, and making your relationship your priority will be more of a reality.

Key #2

Love is a Verb, So Focus on the Action

"Love is a decision followed by a million loving actions."
—Harville Hendrix, PhD

Most couples claim to love one another and think they are behaving in a manner that signals love to their partner. But, if most couples actually do love their partners and believe their actions convey that love, why do so many people secretly or openly wonder if their partner loves them? If the simple fact of loving one another is enough, then why do people argue so much in order to get their needs met? Confusing stuff!

Love means many things at different times in the course of a long-term relationship. In the early stages of a relationship, we believe we love one another, but every couple who has remained together for 10-plus years knows that early phase wasn't "real love" but "infatuation." As we discussed in the first chapter, Mother Nature wired humans to start romantic relationships with fireworks in order to make a couple behave in ways that stoke the fire of passion and forge connection. As relationships develop, however, everyone moves into the inevitable, more challenging phase. Remember that the relationship challenge phase isn't about dominance but about whose preferences, opinions, viewpoints, traditions, styles, and approach will be implemented. Again, that struggle for influence is a natural, unavoidable phase—not a bad thing. If left to become a long-term negative pattern of conflict, however, the relationship challenge phase can demolish the best of relationships!

To keep your relationships strong, you have to become *intentional* in how you treat your partner. When you are bickering about who is right, you stop treating one another as lovers and friends. You have to remember that *love is a verb* and discipline yourself to practice *actions of love*. What nature once did for you, you must do now on your own if you intend to make love last.

In this chapter, we will look at the verb love and teach you how to use *loving actions* to make your relationship not only rock solid but also so joyful, sweet, meaningful, and fun that you can't wait to get home to each other.

Part 1

Learn Love's Ways

"Love thy partner as she or he wants to be loved."

—Harville Hendrix PhD

Nature gave you a taste of passion and connection in the beginning of your relationship. Think of that taste as a movie trailer of coming attractions. You got tantalizing glimpses of how great your movie could be—minus the boring parts, bad acting, and hard-to-follow plot—so you would "commit" to watching the whole thing. But to see the whole movie of your relationship and really enjoy it, you would have to make a further investment: actually help to finish the script, play a role, show up for the screening, and surrender yourself to the emotional experience.

In the infatuation phase of a relationship, "being in love" translates into, "I have found my twin and we will agree with one another forever!" and "I love the way I feel around you. I am stronger, smarter, prettier, more handsome, funnier, and more lovable in your presence." The feeling seems like real love because the communication and connection is so easy and effortless; there's no hard work of explaining yourself or accepting your partner's viewpoint. As you automatically make your relationship the priority of your lives in this phase, you and your partner offer unlimited access to each other's time. You affirm one another's thoughts and feelings in order to show your love. You give and accept appreciation and gifts. And whatever and however your lover expresses his/her affection is "just right."

Love at this point also translates into, "I want your body more than I have ever wanted anything." The powerful hormones of infatuation supercharge your testosterone levels, raising them above their normal baseline. So you reach out more. You touch, caress, and hold hands. You make and accept sexual overtures. And you do this effortlessly. Your walls are down, and with those walls go your inhibitions. You show your physical love easily and often.

When you are falling in love, you also express "I love you" in a multitude of ways that basically boil down to, "I am coming to depend on your love. I am *attached* to you." That is exactly what Mother Nature wants for you, attachment to a worthy partner. All those small actions and words—the expression of love the verb—are designed to bond a couple. The thoughtfulness, the fulfillment of anticipated needs, the gifts, the sex, the fun, and laughter, they're all nature's means of bonding couples so they will stay together to raise offspring.

The drive to bond doesn't care if we don't want to raise children or can't or are too old to reproduce. The successful early humans were the ones who could form a strong attachment and dependency on others and tolerate another's dependency upon them. We are their descendants, and we inherited those genes.

So, when we are courting and infatuation is in charge, we automatically do all the things that forge our connection, strengthen our attachment, and fuel our dependency. This is healthy and necessary for the survival of a relationship. The trouble lies ahead when we are naïve to the fact that we must take deliberate actions in order to continue what nature so generously started.

The Relationship Challenge Phase: From Delight to Disappointment

What causes the blinders of infatuation are all the intoxicating endorphins released in the bloodstream when we fall in love. The chemicals make us feel "high" and whole, but they only last for about 16 to 18 months. Then Nature's drugs begin to fade and the blinders are removed—and you will have to continue the effort of keeping one another happy, while "sober." That's a lot harder to do.

As noted earlier, this relationship challenge phase usually begins when you say, "I do," and move in together. Nature has accomplished its goal of pairing you with another person, and now you have to figure out how to live together for life. So your differences are bound to surface.

During the relationship challenge phase, you don't feel as wonderful or excited as during the infatuation phase. You may see your partner as withholding, protesting, or reacting defensively. You may begin to hear complaints such as "Why don't you talk with me?" or "Why are you always_____?" (Fill in the blank with whatever nagging, critical, or judgmental questions you can imagine.) And, most importantly, your behavior may be deteriorating as well.

Unconsciously, this can activate unfinished business from childhood. Whether it is pain caused by an absent parent or anger, criticism, blaming or shaming from a guardian, we all experienced some degree of difficulty growing up. As children, we all needed an attuned parent and protective boundaries. If we received these, we thrived. If we did not, we had to find a way to survive.

We carry this "baggage" into our committed relationships, and, when our partner disappoints us in a similar way, we move into our protective behaviors with some form of protest, withdrawal, collapse, or stonewalling. When the conflict begins and the old disappointments are activated, we stop trying as hard to show our partner love. We are hurt and confused, and in this state we stop being sensitive and creative.

Even in the good times between conflicts, our lack of awareness causes us to make mistakes in how we show love. We fall prey to assuming we know what our partner wants; to resisting giving because we feel manipulated; to having issues with our own poor self-esteem; and to simmering resentment and judgments. Without understanding the unconscious processes at work—and without having the skills to consciously take command of a deteriorating situation—what once felt like a romantic comedy rapidly becomes a dark drama.

Learning what our partner needs and overcoming our own obstacles to giving and receiving takes work. It requires us to learn how to love our partner. When we make the decision to do this and follow it with actions and behaviors that meet our partner's needs, that's when we find real love. And when we experience real love, we make our relationship rock solid.

How Will You Know What Makes Your Partner Feel Loved? Ask!

Our attempt to give our partner love is often based on our own ideas of what love is rather than on our partner's ideas. Remember, in the infatuation phase, we thought we married our twin, and we unconsciously believe we see the world the same way and think alike. When we enter the relationship challenge phase, this thinking backfires, and the result is misunderstanding, disappointment, and conflict.

Years ago, Tim's wife threw him a surprise birthday party with a several of his friends. Tim loved it so much that he did the same for her birthday. Imagine how surprised he was when she was not happy. She told him she didn't like to be the center of attention. She would have preferred a nice dinner with another couple. The mistake Tim made was giving from his own frame of reference, instead of knowing what made her feel loved.

The interesting thing about this relationship challenge phase is that it's supposed to happen. You are with another person who is not just like you. You discover, sometimes painfully, that you have differences. Tim's wife is a distinct person with truly unique thoughts, feelings, and viewpoints. Tim had to learn which actions she needed in order to feel loved.

This can be discouraging when we have grown up hearing messages from our parents, church, friends, fairytales, and the media that tell us essentially that, if we really love our partner, we would just *know* what he or she needs in order to feel love. Movies, songs, stories, and fairytales tell us that couples meet, fall in love, and live happily ever after. But how does this happen? Are we supposed to "mind read" what will make our partners fall in love and be happy?

You may have already figured out that guessing what your partner needs is a bad idea that can lead to a lot of frustration on both your parts. Sure, you may get lucky and hit the bull's eye with a guess, but then it's technically possible that you'll win the lottery, too. The point is, the odds are stacked against you. When you guess, you come from your own frame of reference instead of your partner's. So, what can you do? Ask.

Ask your partner what feels loving, and, when he/she responds, listen and take notes. For example, you might inquire, "Please tell me 10 things I can do or have done to make you feel loved." Then ask your partner to listen to, or read, the list *you* compile of what you would like your partner to do to make *you* happy. Sounds simple, but it can be difficult to do. Why is this so hard? Because cultural messages tell us we should "just know," and we feel discomfort or shame when we don't. The truth is that we don't know what our partner wants and needs, and it is his/her responsibility as an adult to learn to tell us—and for us to ask. (The reverse is also true.) You didn't pair up with someone just like yourself. No one does. Healthy relationships require communicating about what we each need to feel happy.

After each of you has the list of what each enjoys as loving behaviors, resolve to do one or two daily. Then, in a month, compare how each of you is doing. With more experience, you and your partner can adjust your lists and become experts at expressing real love. This will move you a long way toward a rock solid relationship.

Part 2

Act with Love Regularly

"Practice daily acts of random kindness and frequent terms of endearment and tailor them to your relationship."

—Bruce Lipton, PhD

By now we hope you understand that love needs to be made anew every day. In fact, the joyous responsibility of a committed relationship is that you will show your love actively at least a few times a day.

Acting with love comes in three sizes: small, medium, and large. Small actions are the daily loving behaviors such as the welcome home kiss, a sweet text in the middle of the day, bringing your partner a cup of coffee, and an appreciation spoken earnestly. Medium actions take more planning and effort. These would include date nights, a surprise gift, making love, buying tickets to a concert, or setting aside time for fun. Large actions require advanced planning, lots of discussion, and perhaps saving money. Examples are weekends spent away, an overnight hike, vacations without the kids, and major adventures. Large size undertakings often involve checking something off your bucket list.

The actions of love can be grouped into several categories:

- Accepting Your Partner

- Tenderness and Affection

- Affirmation, Appreciations and Encouragement

- Acts of Responsibility

- Acts of Giving

- Couple Time

- Keeping Romance Alive

- Sex

In this section, we will talk about the first seven. Sex is such an important category of love in action that we devote an entire chapter to its discussion.

Accepting Your Partner

Nothing says love as much as feeling accepted by one's partner. To accept your partner means a number of things. Many of the Oxford dictionary's definitions of the verb *accept* are beautiful concepts for a couple to consider. *To accept* is, "to take willingly something that is offered," "to agree to or approve of something," "to make somebody feel welcome," and "to receive something as *good enough.*"

In general, accepting your partner involves acknowledging that he/she is an individual with his/her way of seeing and doing things, that he/she is just as OK as you are, and that his/her ideas are not inferior to your own. To accept your partner is to allow his/her point of view to prevail—at least half the time—without a fuss or anxiety that his/her way will not be good enough.

Most of us are guilty of "My way is the right way" thinking. In reality, your way is *your* way and your partner's way is just as valid! And, no, it isn't your job to change your partner's mind about every little thing.

When Norene was first married, she couldn't tolerate the way her husband made the bed. Never mind that he was making the bed without any prompting from Norene; he wasn't making it the *right* way. In her mind, only one correct way to make a bed existed—the way her mom insisted the job be done. Period. She continued to "constructively" criticize Tom's method, showing him the things he was doing wrong. He continued to maintain that his way of making the bed was just fine. The discomfort was so bad for Norene that she couldn't sleep well in the bed if it weren't made up right! We aren't talking about the sheets being too tight or the blankets, too few. We are talking appearances here. Norene had a strong need to assert her point of view—and to have that point of view prevail in the marriage. Bless his heart, Tom just kept making the bed and didn't let Norene's bickering stop him. One day, they shared the escalating struggle with a marriage counselor who pointed out that there isn't a universally correct way to make a bed—that, in fact, Norene simply *preferred* her way. Both partners each had an equally valid opinion about bed making; neither of them had the only correct opinion. Once Norene accepted that Tom did, in fact, have a valid point of view and that she wasn't right, she and Tom could go about figuring out how to work with their differing styles.

As noted earlier, being accepted by your partner is a wonderful expression of love. When you acknowledge that your partner's way of thinking, feeling, and acting is as good as your own, your partner can relax and be open and passionate in return. When you seek your partner's opinion and let that opinion prevail half the time, you are showing you accept his or her intelligence, wisdom, and creativity. Imagine how loved your partner will feel when you are willing to make ample space for his or her full self in your relationship!

Tenderness and Affection

In addition to accepting your partner—in all his or her quirky, complicated, interesting, odd wonder—being affectionate and tender also can be instrumental in bringing the two of you closer and in fortifying your relationship. Acts of tenderness and affection may or may not be sensual in nature. Even small, romantic gestures can help you to bond. We are talking about the kind of intimate touches and actions suitable in public—even though these acts may at times lead to sex. They might include holding hands, giving a back rub, lingering hugs, opening doors, kissing for the heck of it, or driving with your hand on your partner's knee. Even spontaneously dancing together while you clean the kitchen is an affectionate act.

Sending emails, voicemails, and texts are another way to show tenderness, but they only count if used in conjunction with physical expressions. A quick message saying, "Love you and miss you. Can't wait to see you tonight" definitely conveys affection, but technology will never be as valuable to a marriage as physical affection. It can only *supplement* a good old-fashioned touch or hug.

In fact, research indicates that one 10-second hug a day can lead to hormonal reactions in your body that can significantly improve your health. According to one study, the improvement includes reducing stress, easing depression, and boosting the immune system (Forsell and Åström, 2012). Also, one 20-second hug per day increases blood levels of the "love hormone," oxytocin; oxytocin bonds couples and encourages trust (Dobson, 2012). If one hug per day can accomplish this much, imagine what hugging one another four times per day could do to make you both feel important, loved, and even healthier!

Flirting, too, is wonderful, because it makes your partner feel good. Don't confuse flirting with teasing, though. Teasing doesn't always land as affection. Flirting does. Flirting is the tilt of your head, the arch of the eyebrow, and a look or words that convey, "You are pretty darn cute and I want your attention."

As you re-energize this area of showing love, be sensitive to the impact on your partner. If your partner expresses or indicates discomfort with a gesture, pay attention and stop showing love in that particular way. Don't take the feedback personally, because it is not personal. What your partner thinks, feels, and does is about them, *not you*. He or she is entitled to his/her preferences in love, especially where touch is concerned, just as you are.

Talk openly about the gestures of tenderness and affection you both prefer. Does your partner enjoy it when you lift her hair and kiss her neck? Or perhaps she loves those times you put your hand on the small of her back when you are walking. Maybe he enjoys having his shoulders rubbed for a few minutes when he is at the computer. Or his favorite gesture could be a back scratch.

Every day without fail, give your partner at least two gestures of affection and tenderness. This tip for putting love into action won't take up more than a few minutes of time! Hopefully, this is one area in which you will enjoy both giving and receiving equally.

Affirm, Appreciate, and Encourage

Do you tell your partner at least once per day you think he or she is terrific? Do you let him or her know how valuable he or she is to you—and why? Verbal appreciations are a means of "catching your partner doing the right thing" and are vital to healthy relationships.

Too often, we do not spend enough time affirming, showing gratitude, or cheering on a partner. Instead, we tend to fill up the airtime with "directions or corrections." Directions are statements such as, "I need you to go to the store for me" or "Please discipline the kids." These directions are generally benign requests for help, but they can be delivered with a tone that makes the direction sound like a demand. Corrections are expressions of an opinion. Whether delivered lightly or harshly, corrections are basically complaints. Nothing is inherently wrong with directions and corrections. When done too frequently, however, they turn into nagging. The sad and dangerous fact is that many couples only communicate in directions and corrections.

Consider the value of adding daily verbal expressions of appreciation and encouragement. Think how much happier the environment between the two of you could be if you spoke up daily and said, "Thanks for unloading the dishwasher." "Wow, you are the best cook in the world." "I love you more than anyone or anything." "You can do that marathon. I know you can. I want to be there along the way cheering you on." "You smell great." "You are the most handsome man in the world." See where we are going with this? *You are the representative of adult love for your partner.* He or she looks to you for approval all the time, both consciously and unconsciously. Too much disapproval can kill a relationship. It makes us feel unworthy. Everyone needs validation, cheerleading, and expressions of respect in order to feel our best.

Interestingly, a common misconception is that people are supposed to generate 100% of their own feelings of approval and not look outside for affirmation. Nothing could be further from the truth. Our human ancestors looked to each other for approval and acceptance in order to assess their behavior, and those traits have continued on in us. Feeling most comfortable when we know the people we love and depend upon are happy with our behavior is hardwired in each of us.

Your partner unconsciously looks to you for acceptance. You are the one who should be noticing your partner's beauty and strength. You are the one who sees his or her struggles and should offer encouragement. You are also the one who reaps the benefits of the actions taken by your partner to support your lifestyle. So speak up! Affirm, appreciate, and encourage. Eventually, verbal expressions of love will become second nature.

Acts of Responsibility

The last category about verbal expressions was about *speaking up*. This one is about *getting up*… and doing things responsibly. Showing responsibility in your relationship is a major category of love as a verb. Sharing a home, perhaps children, and a family life requires equal partnership in order to build a strong marriage. With a lot to be done, a strong couple must define and share responsibilities—and thank each other for being responsible.

Responsible actions are only a loving gesture if they are done willingly and without nagging. Make a list of every responsibility in your marriage you can define. Go beyond the obvious housework and laundry. Include things such as ordering and stacking firewood, cleaning the gutters, buying school clothes and birthday gifts, taking the kids to dentist appointments, etc. Share your lists and talk about how often the activities must be done and who usually does them. Do you like the tasks and responsibilities you have? Does the current way of doing things work for both of you? Do both of you feel the breakdown of responsibility is equal in the ways that you each want it to be equal?

In order for this category to be defined as an act of love, you must both take on your fair share. Acts of responsibility aren't always fun. You may not always want to shop for groceries, but, if you agree to shop, then holding up your part of the bargain is an expression of *love as a verb*. It says to your partner, "Because you mean so much to me, you can count on me to do as I promised and go to the market so our basic needs will be met." These types of actions tell your partner that his or her comfort and happiness is important to you. In order for these actions to convey love, they must be done in a timely manner as you promised. This requires that you act like an adult, and that you allow your partner to be an adult.

Once you divide up the tasks in a manner that seems fair to you both, you need to agree on when the tasks should be done and how often. In dividing the chores, consider which ones you feel *must* be done your way. Harkening back to Norene's story about how a bed "should be made," if it is important to you that your style of doing the chore prevails, you should take on that chore. You are both adults and you need to respect that your partner has opinions and styles different from your own. To minimize conflict, consider any strong preferences when you divide up the responsibilities. In dividing them, do what actually works for you two.

Consider the example of Ben and Dawn, who, for several years, tried to divide things neutrally and not based on gender. But the truth is, Dawn didn't want to be the one who cleans gutters, and Ben didn't enjoy planning menus. Finally, they evolved to doing what they most enjoyed or felt strongly about and sharing the ones they didn't, such as that dreaded bathroom cleaning.

Once you have divided up the chores, you have to follow through. To do so is to be a responsible adult. Responsible adults do what they have promised to do, or they come to one another right away and explain delays. This works both ways. Letting your partner be a responsible adult means you give him or her the opportunity to develop an individual approach to the chores or tasks at hand. It doesn't have to be your way when your partner performs the task, nor does he or she have to do them entirely upon your schedule. That's controlling, not loving.

People always will feel especially loved when their partner spontaneously engages in acts of responsibility. For example, perhaps your partner sometimes washes your car, not because it is his or her job, but because he or she wants to make you feel happy and pleased. If you are among those lucky enough to have a partner who, out of pure love, showers you with small, but significant acts of kindness, you need to acknowledge the gift! Show your partner you are pleased and grateful. These categories of showing love fit together! One partner does something loving, and the receiving partner notices and appreciates.

If your partner doesn't notice your action, don't take it personally. It could be for lots of reasons. It is not uncommon throughout a long marriage to miss some of your partner's kindnesses. We do take one another for granted, and we need to become more conscious and develop better habits of paying attention. If you ever find yourself in the situation of an act of kindness or responsibility going unnoticed, instead of being hurt, just sweetly point out the kindness: "Hey, did you notice your clean car?" There is nothing wrong with drawing attention to your action. After all, you are learning to work together as a team, showing and accepting love.

Acts of Giving

Our next category is gifts and generosity. It could have the subtitle, "Love is a Four-Letter Word Spelled G-I-V-E."

As marriage counselors for decades, we have seen some of the worst pain come from a partner ignoring anniversaries, birthdays, or holidays. A back-story about what happened always exists, but partners can feel wounded if we do not actively give tokens of love. Gifts do not have to be big, expensive, or "perfect," but you should take the time to find gifts your partner will enjoy. Every anniversary deserves at least a love letter written in a thoughtfully chosen or self-created card. Every birthday deserves a special meal, a toast, or a thoughtful gift. Every holiday deserves a special expression of appreciation and care.

Forget the pressure to purchase luxury items and expensive jewelry. But also forget the neckties and toasters. Really think about what your partner would find touching. Consider restaurant gift certificates with a coupon for a night out with you. Listen to your partner's interests in books or music and make note so, when an occasion rolls around, you have something in mind.

Although special occasions should be acknowledged with a generosity of heart, some of the best gifts are given spontaneously. If you see a cookie in a bakery you know your partner would enjoy, then bring it home and place it on a plate for dessert. This surprise thoughtfulness says, "I think about you when I am not with you."

When gifts are given, it is crucial you receive them well. Frequently, people are disappointed by the gifts chosen by their partner. Enough years of gifts being "wrong" only trains your partner to stop giving out of fear of rejection. If this is an issue for you, ask yourself why gifts must be perfect?

What is the story you tell yourself when you are given a gift you don't like? Do you personalize the wrong choice and think your partner just doesn't get you or that he/she wants to disappoint you on purpose? Now ask yourself, where did that line of thinking come from? What childhood memories do you have, good or bad, about the giving of gifts? Could this baggage be interfering with your enjoying what your partner gives? If your partner buys you clothes that do not fit or aren't flattering, then have a talk at a time you aren't in the middle of receiving a gift. Explain you are picky about clothes and prefer always to choose them for yourself but that, instead, you would appreciate a gift card for your favorite department store.

Couple Time

As noted in the last chapter, spending time together makes a significant "deposit in the relationship savings account." Some examples of things to do during your time together include just talking, going on a date, having an adventure, playing a game, doing a project, occasionally watching a show, relaxing in the hot tub, taking a walk, cuddling, or maybe even making love. But couple time is only special when you are not distracted —and only effective if just the two of you are involved and the experience is *relational*. That is, going to a movie doesn't count!

Sadly, studies have found that a third of couples spend less than 30 minutes of quality time together each day, and that three in 10 couples feel their relationship is suffering due to the lack of couple time (From *Love by Numbers*, Luisa Dillner, quoting Office of National Statistics, Great Britain, 2004). Remember, love is a verb. You cannot use your words alone. You must also take action. And couple time is a big action.

You may verbalize your love to your partner, but, if you don't spend time connecting when you're alone and focused, your marriage is empty. At least once a day you need couple time. Even 20 minutes together interacting will strengthen your connection. Don't say you can't manage your time so you can climb into bed together regularly. It's not true. Turn off televisions and computers and go to bed at the same time at least three nights per week. Have a weekly date night. Set aside weekly times to play a game or go for a walk. You get the point! Your relationship must be your number one priority if you want your love to last.

An important part of couple time needs to be talking to each other. In our offices we have noted what many studies have found, that one in four couples speak to their partner for less than 10 minutes a day (O'Connor, 2005). If you and your partner are in that statistic, no good can come of it. That level of disconnection will weaken your marriage. Studies also have shown that couples who average over 30 minutes per day talking with each other have a significantly higher rate of happiness (O'Connor, 2005). And, please, no sitting in the living room ignoring the living, breathing spouse beside you while you take the time to update your social media site! Otherwise, you soon may be changing your Facebook status to single.

Long-married, happy, and engaged couples tell us that they talk to their spouses as much as time allows. They say they can't get enough conversation with their spouses, because they don't get bored and they look forward to sharing everything. In decades of marriage, they have learned to share their thoughts and feelings—and they have learned to make it safe for their partners to share their thoughts and feelings.

One more note on talking daily during couple time. Talking is foreplay for a very important loving action: sex. The more we share our thoughts, feelings, experiences, dreams, hopes, and fears, the closer we feel. The closer we feel, the more we want to touch one another. Talking is the gateway to sex. Open the gate.

Keep Romance Alive

What is romance? It is the delicious feeling of anticipation and mystery associated with an intimate relationship. It is the experience of feeling that your partner wants to surprise you, please you, and thrill you. Romantic overtures show you your partner has been thinking of you when you were apart. They show that you two are lovers, special, and not just friends. Romance has elements of fun, spontaneity, sensuality, and discovery.

All romantic relationships start with making romance a priority. Once again, the chemicals make us "do it." Although no relationship can sustain the infatuation phase for more than a matter of months, you can keep romance alive for a lifetime. And you must if you want your relationship to be rock solid.

Both men and women have romantic expectations. If you don't continue the regular efforts necessary to meet those expectations, you and your partner will be disappointed. Also, consider this, no one else can meet your partner's romantic expectations. At least you do not want them to be met by others. You and your partner are the sole source for romance and for sex (but more on that later). If you do not make adequate efforts toward romance, you both will feel romantic deprivation.

There is a popular myth that men don't like romantic gestures; almost every sitcom has numerous episodes in which a clueless man is flummoxed by his female partner's need for romance. Ugh! Hollywood! A man's real need for romance is just as significant as a woman's. In a large research study of couples worldwide, men indicated they needed more romance in their relationship at the same percentage as women did. In fact, the study found that more than a third of the men throughout the world said they were bothered their partner wasn't more romantic (Northrup, Schwartz, and Witte, 2014).

Dates can be an important source of romance. Regular dates and fun activities boost intimacy and happiness. Couples who continue to date once per week over the course of their marriage are three times more likely to report feeling happy in their marriages than those couples who have stopped having a date night (Foster, 2012). Dates don't need to be expensive, but they need to be regular and consistent. Many obstacles can get in the way of dating including, money, time, and children. Be honest with yourself! You could probably find the money for toys that will end up in the back of your child's closet, for a big screen television, or for a new sweater or shirt. To find the time to date, simply turn off all screens and get your chores done so you can go out and have fun! As for the kids, establish regular date nights early in your relationship and get creative with childcare trades and babysitter sharing.

Research has always shown that couples who have regular dates have the highest sexual frequency and are less likely to divorce (Foster, 2012). You can't beat that, can you? Well, apparently you can—by double dating with another couple. Going on a double date can reignite passion in your relationship even better than a candlelit dinner for two. According to new research, socializing with another couple in which you discuss personal details of your life will bring you closer to your own partner (Society for Personality and Social Psychology, 2014). Time spent with another couple sharing thoughts and experiences puts your spouse in a new light. You learn things from his or her disclosures, as well as see what a funny, sensitive, and likable person he or she can be.

Sharing personally doesn't necessarily mean sharing intimate details of conflict or sexuality. In the research study, when people shared about such topics as "What is your idea of a perfect day?" or "Given the choice of anyone in the world, whom would you want as a dinner guest?" the couples reported feeling closer to and more attracted to their partner (same study as above). Seeing your sweetie interact openly, candidly, humorously, and in an animated style makes you remember why you fell in love with him or her in the first place.

As important as dating is, romantic gestures shouldn't be limited to date nights. When planning more romantic actions, remember that *romance and sex are two different things*. Making love can be very romantic, but even more romantic can be a kiss on the back of the neck, or holding your partner and telling him or her how great he or she smells. Romantic gestures also do not have to be costly. Consider these inexpensive examples gleaned from books and the Internet. Because men and women state slightly different romantic preferences, we have separated them into gender categories.

Romantic Ideas for Her

- Send regular cards and love letters. If you aren't a big writer, spend the time necessary to find cards that actually express how you feel. Mail the cards to her, even if you live with her.

- Draw a "frame" on the bathroom mirror with a bar of soap and write, "picture perfect" beneath it.

- Surprise her with a picnic lunch complete with a blanket, a basket of deli foods, and some music.

- Put rose petals all over the bed.

- Leave her a short love note in the back pages of a book she is reading.

- Leave her a single red rose under the windshield wipers, on her pillow, at the computer, or at her dinner plate. Don't include a note. The rose says it all.

- Take a picture of yourself holding a sign that says, "I Love You!" and post it on her Facebook page.

- On a moonless night, take her stargazing. Take along a blanket, pillows, wine (be the designated driver so she can enjoy more than a glass), and a wonderful dessert from her favorite place.

- Show her affection in public. Hold her hand, put your arm around her, open a car door, and spontaneously give her a kiss on the street or trail.

Romantic Ideas for Him

- Join him in his hobby spontaneously. Play a video game. Bring him dessert from your girl's night out.

- Greet him at the door and give him a real kiss. Not a peck on the cheek. A movie kiss!

- Give him a massage without his having to ask.

- Have a Happy Hour at Home awaiting him. Make cocktails and appetizers or open a bottle of wine and prepare an antipasti plate.

- Plan a date and pay for it.

- Write him a card telling him he is handsome and caring and you'll love him no matter what. Underline the words, "You make me so happy." Mail it to him at work if you can. If not, mail it to your home.

- Take his arm when you cross the street.

- Take him out for a drink and sit near him. Whisper something in his ear, not blatantly sexual, but romantic or promising.

- Get the kids out of the house for the night, get his favorite comedy, make homemade popcorn, buy his favorite movie candy and beverage, and light some candles. Sit close, play footsies, and laugh with him. (No heavy talk!)

- Committed relationships need romance like a flower needs water. Nothing will make you as beloved by your partner as continued romantic efforts and gestures.

Part 3

What Gets in the Way of Giving Your Partner What He or She Really Wants?

"When you say 'I love you,' you are making a promise with someone else's heart. You should honor it with actions to prove it. Love is not only an emotion. Love is a verb."

—Unknown

Missing Skills

In order to put love into action, you need a certain skill set you either learned or didn't learn in your childhood. As children, we all received messages about what was okay or not okay to think and feel and do. We witnessed the adults in our lives and unconsciously modeled ourselves to be like them. Or, we shaped ourselves in reaction to them in order to be totally different.

Regardless, as children we develop only the skills that our parents find acceptable and important. The skills and behaviors that were deemed unacceptable or unimportant were not developed. So we arrive at adulthood with a skill set from childhood that may be missing proficiencies in several areas.

An amazing effect of the infatuation phase is that you were attracted to and became involved with someone who has the missing skills you didn't develop. Likewise, your partner chose you because you have his or her missing skills. Once infatuation turns into a committed relationship, you and your partner have the unique and important opportunity to grow and master all the skills that will bring you both joy and fulfillment—but only if you choose to work at it.

If you find that showing love in certain ways is a challenge, don't despair. The key is to let your partner know that his or her request is difficult for you and that some patience, empathy, and encouragement on his or her part would be appreciated.

Let's say you grew up in a family where there was little physical affection. If giving physical affection is not a skill you witnessed or developed growing up, chances are that affection will be the loving action your partner desires most, and he or she may become frustrated if you're not providing it. Committed relationship provides the opportunity to develop our full adult capabilities. If you married someone who never challenges you in your areas of arrested development, you will never grow.

A common misconception is that, if you weren't raised with a particular loving action, it's just not in you. We often hear, "That's not me" or "I wasn't raised that way." The truth is that, even if you haven't developed that loving skill yet, you still can. We are all capable of learning to express our love and grow the skills that our partner desires.

When we learn a new loving skill, we not only make our partner feel loved, but we also become more confident, complete, and fulfilled. With consistent effort, you can learn to give your partner the treatment that spells L-O-V-E to them.

Here's an exercise you can do to develop your loving skills:

- Ask your partner what he or she would like to see more of from you.

- Choose one doable loving action and commit aloud to doing it consistently.

- Check in with your partner on a weekly basis for a month, asking how your efforts are going. Share your own view of this as well, and be sure to include any difficulties you encountered. If modifications are needed, commit to taking new action.

You may be tempted to do several loving actions that your partner would like at the same time. It's better, however, to do just one and learn to do it well so you don't get overwhelmed and stop trying altogether. Your partner will notice your effort, and you will learn the loving skills that will touch your partner's heart.

Self-hate

When you first met your partner and fell in love, you wanted to give him or her everything possible. You intuitively knew what would make your new sweetie happy, and you did it without any self-conscious feelings or inhibitions.

Later in the relationship when the infatuation chemicals subside, lovers find it much harder to give. This is natural, and all of us struggle with it to some extent. If you struggle with it more than you wish, you might consider that your own low self-esteem or even self-hate may be in the way. Why would this be? Because if you don't feel good about yourself and you don't easily accept loving actions, you will not think to do them for your partner.

When you are romantically involved, you become merged with your partner. Your brain isn't even sure where you end and your partner begins. Again, this is normal. Nature wants you to feel that your partner is an extension of you so that you will look after your "other half" as you look after yourself. But, if you don't like yourself or you grew up hearing negative messages about your worth, you are going to neglect yourself and you will neglect your "other half" as well.

One of the great things about life-long relationships is that we have a chance to repair the damage of childhood. If you didn't learn that your wants and needs are important, then your marriage is a chance to learn something new. Practicing asking for what you need and giving your partner what he or she asks for develops a new habit. This new habit will work on your unconscious processes, and you will begin to feel more deserving. Perhaps it will feel uncomfortable or awkward, but every new habit feels that way at first.

Feeling Manipulated

It is fairly common that one or both partners can feel manipulated by the other. So, what's wrong with manipulation? All people try to arrange a situation for a favorable outcome. The problem is that, at times, your partner will feel coerced by your attempts to have your needs or opinions prevail. Even on small things, your partner might feel unequal or cornered by your tactics. This can come from small actions where one of you wants your way about something, to a full-blown pattern where negativity, resentment, conflict, and distance can lead to the demise of the relationship.

When you are newly committed to your relationship, feeling manipulated can signal the start of your relationship challenges. Suppose your partner gives you an expensive new set of skis, and you don't like to ski. You tried it back in college and never really enjoyed it. Your partner thinks he will get you to like it. You just need to try it; he is sure you'll come around to love skiing. So, you try to ski. You discover you are cold, you fall a lot, and the speed going downhill scares you. Your partner is now frustrated that you haven't grown to love skiing, and you are now resentful that he tried to get you to like it. As resentment builds, those skis sit in the garage.

Shortly after making a commitment, couples begin to experience feeling manipulated. You both have an image of what you want in your relationship and that image is of a person who wants everything the way you want it to be. Independent perspectives and preferences are normal, and all of us are capable of manipulation because it is an unconscious attempt to get our needs met. It's not that you are bad or want control; it's that you have feelings, needs, and wants you don't know how to deal with on a conscious level. An example is our skiing enthusiast above. The partner who wanted his partner to go skiing had a desire. It just wasn't his partner's desire. If they had a safe conversation and learned about each other, a lot of frustration could have been avoided.

Commitment is about learning that you and your partner are different—and navigating those differences in a way that builds trust, connection, and companionship. Problems occur when negative attempts to get your needs met become entrenched patterns and resentment builds. Learning to navigate your relationship without manipulation will build respect, equality, and appreciation. You can overcome feeling manipulated and being manipulative with the help of effective communication skills and a little effort.

Remember that everyone is, at times, manipulative. Sometimes we are aware of what we are doing; other times we are acting unconsciously. All couples resort to manipulative attempts to get their needs met when they do not know how to ask directly. Being direct without blame is a challenge, but it is a vital ingredient in making your marriage rock solid. Using skilled communication such as the Intentional Dialogue we will introduce in Key #4 can help you both to express your needs clearly and hear your partner's needs without over reacting. The result will be that you will both feel understood and equal, and the feeling of manipulation will subside.

Standoffs

One definition of *real love* is: "doing something you don't want to do for someone you don't particularly like at that moment." Inside both you and your partner is a little kid guilty of having both prideful and hurt feelings. After months or years of poor treatment, you may feel it isn't fair you have to give—anything. "What about him?" or "She should go first!" are common "standoff" comments.

You can live your day-to-day life in a standoff, holding out on your partner until he or she "goes first." What that will lead to will be either long-term misery or divorce. The other alternative is to take the high road and reach out first. Once the ball is rolling again between the two of you, does it really matter who started? Do you want to be right—or do you want a happy and loving relationship?

If you feel particularly stuck or stubborn, start with two loving actions per day *that you can manage*. Perhaps you don't feel you can give your partner a tender kiss, but we bet you could greet them in the morning with a smile and offer a cup of coffee. Do these two loving actions consistently for a week. When you realize that giving was not as hard as you thought, add a few more. We think you will see reciprocal responses coming from your partner before long. If you do not get an in-kind response, return to the list of loving actions you made with your partner. Remember to make certain that the loving actions you are giving come from your partner's list and not from your idea of what love should be.

Negative Judgments

Have you ever had moments when you realized you treat your partner worse or more harshly than you treat others? Relationship counselors have often thought that all couples suffer from some trouble with letting another person really close. This makes sense, because no one had a perfect childhood, and we were all hurt to some extent. To paraphrase the words of Harville Hendrix, the author of *Getting the Love You Want*, we are born in a relationship, we are wired and wounded in relationships, and we can only be healed in a relationship.

The wiring and wounding of early relationships leaves us each with a unique tolerance for how much closeness we can tolerate. When a partner becomes too close, we feel uncomfortable. After all, he or she may disapprove of us, start a conflict, or boss us around. To manage the discomfort, our brain begins to notice how our partner is different than us. We then unconsciously label the differences as negative, and we judge and criticize in order to justify stepping back and not being as close. It sounds crazy, but it's not. It's human nature. However, treating your partner with love is difficult if you are frequently thinking harsh thoughts.

No matter how often you think negatively about your partner, it would benefit you to incorporate the following simple practice, which can be done anywhere, into your daily routine:

For one minute, close your eyes and picture your partner at his or her most appealing. Maybe you see him in a shirt that makes his eyes shine.

Maybe she's asleep. Or awake. Laughing. Paying attention to you. Making love. Whatever image holds positive feelings for you. Spend just one minute and do this three times a day. In this process, you will rewire your brain for automatic loving thoughts of your partner. You also will increase your hard-wired ability to tolerate closeness.

If you do catch yourself making negative judgments, stop the thought and replace it with three positive statements. If you thought, "He's never on time," replace it with, "He is such a good dad." Over time, you will see an improvement in your mood, and you will find it effortless to give positive energy to your partner.

You may fear this practice is "glossing over" imperfections your partner should improve. Spouses who see their partners with fondness and admiration and express the positive emotions benefit from a longevity bonus of an estimated 10 years (Frederickson, 2013). Even those who fight regularly but see their partner as the greatest thing in the world will tell you they are very happy. What makes them happy is how they see the goodness in their partner and even exaggerate it. But, hey, if you are going to exaggerate your partner's traits, it's better you exaggerate the good ones! (We will discuss more about the danger and damage of negativity in the next chapter.)

Conclusion

Happy couples consistently find ways to express their love throughout the weeks, months, and years, which makes the journey of their lives rich and rewarding. The outcome is that their relationship becomes the bond between them that enlivens their life.

In summary, cultivating a rock solid relationship is accomplished by *making love a verb*. As many great relationship professionals have said, "Love is a decision followed by a million loving actions." We hope the exercises and tips in this chapter have given you some ideas on how exactly to make love a verb. You can always return to the chapter when you need a tune-up. We all need tune-ups from time to time! Do not think you have to master the tools overnight. Small steps done consistently over time create lasting change and real love. Pick something you can do now and make a commitment to start a new loving action today.

For some couples, doing the exercises in this chapter will not be a mutual endeavor. It is normal to question, "Can I succeed in improving our relationship if my partner does not join me in the effort?" The answer is a resounding "yes." When you increase your loving behaviors, your partner will ultimately want to reciprocate. Why? Because when we are given love, it is in our human nature to want to give back. It may take a while, but it will be worth it.

It is also important to note that everyone has defenses or protective behaviors that are not easily overcome. These get in the way of acting lovingly. If your relationship is struggling and at a standoff even after trying our suggested exercises, you may need to seek professional help from a qualified relationship counselor or coach. Contrary to our cultural beliefs, seeking help is a sign of courage and strength. It signals that you are committed to strengthening your marriage. With guidance, loving support, and a commitment to create a great relationship, you can succeed at expressing love in ways you didn't think were possible—and making your love last.

Reflection

When you met your partner, what qualities did he or she possess that made you feel you had found the right person?

When the romantic chemistry wore off and you became disappointed, how did you begin to behave that lead to conflict, discord, or unhappiness? Don't look at your partner's bad behavior here. Look at your own.

Which of the categories of loving actions is your favorite? Which is your partner's favorite? First take a guess, and then ask to learn if you were correct. Rate your own willingness to give each of these with some frequency:

- *Accepting Your Partner*
- *Tenderness and Affection*
- *Affirmation, Appreciations, and Encouragement*

- *Acts of Responsibility*
- *Acts of Giving*
- *Couple Time*
- *Keeping Romance Alive*

What loving actions are you willing to put back into your relationship, regardless of the response?

How are you at receiving love? Do you have any unhelpful old "scripts" that tell you that you don't deserve love? If so, what support might you need to rewrite those scripts?

In what ways do you ask for what you need? Is manipulation one of those ways?

Write a paragraph describing your ideal relationship with your partner in regard to "love, the verb." What would you both be doing more to show love? Then share your paragraph with your partner and discuss his or her reaction. Caution: Don't make the paragraph or discussion all about what your partner can do differently. Make it about "we." For example, you might write, "We have weekly date nights," "We make love every week," or "We tell each other appreciations every day."

Key #3

Negativity Kills Love, So Cut it Out!

"You can measure the happiness of a marriage by the number of scars that each partner carries on their tongues, earned from years of biting back angry words."

—Elizabeth Gilbert

The number one requirement for creating a relationship that's strong enough to last is an atmosphere of safety. And nothing prevents your partner from feeling safe more than does negative treatment.

Most marriage experts agree that negativity kills love. Well-regarded marriage researcher and author Dr. John Gottman has shown that he can predict whether or not a marriage will survive by observing a couple in his clinic for all of five minutes! With an accuracy rate of over 90%, Gottman's studies conclude that couples who were negative during conflict or had a lack of positive emotions in events of the day would eventually divorce. We simply cannot have the connection we long for, or the longevity we desire, when we are thinking or behaving negatively toward our partner. Bottom line: safety and negativity are incompatible!

The Negative Response Cycle . . . and Interrupting It

What is negativity in a relationship? According to Dr. Harville Hendrix, author of *Getting the Love You Want,* negativity is any thought, behavior, or word that tells your partner, "You are not okay when you think the way you think or act the way you act." This message, in effect, rejects your partner's individuality and results in your partner feeling hurt, disrespected—and unsafe. Even if your behavior is a misguided attempt to make a connection with your partner, your negativity will push him or her away. The reason this happens is that negativity triggers defensiveness. That is, your poor behavior will evoke your partner's defensiveness. Who wouldn't counter blame and shame or insults and criticism by getting angry, withdrawing, or shutting down?

Called by Gottman the "Negative Response Cycle," this pattern can be explained through interpersonal neurobiology, or brain science. A "sentinel" in our brain, called the amygdala, stands watch and is prepared to defend us when it spots danger. When we feel anxiety regarding our partner, the amygdala interprets this as danger, and then we defend ourselves. The worse part of this in a marriage is that, when you criticize your partner, his or her amygdala will interpret the situation as, "There is an enemy in the house!" Is that what you want your beloved to feel—that, in the sanctuary of your home, a danger lurks, and that danger is *you?*"

Negativity is not only a form of partner abuse but self-abuse as well. Studies show that, when you yell at your partner, the stress hormone cortisol dramatically increases for both of you. We think this holds true for criticism, blame, and shame as well. The brain doesn't know whether the negativity is going outward or inward, so it dumps cortisol to protect us.

In essence, when partners begin to criticize, blame, shame, belittle, dismiss, avoid, use sarcasm, or condemn each other, they are putting toxins into their relationship that will eventually kill their love for one another. Warning: Even if you didn't intend for a comment to be insulting, if your partner hears it as negative or as a putdown, then it is negative. Period. At that particular moment and in that particular instance, no amount of defending yourself will bring back safety and connection. When a pattern of continual conflict or avoidance creeps into the relationship, no one feels safe—and defensiveness, distance, and loss of intimacy is the outcome.

Interestingly, Dr. Hendrix theorizes that negativity toward a partner is our "adult cry." Think about when you were a baby. What did you do when you needed something? Did you say to your parents, "Hey, I'm hungry! Can you feed me?" Or did you cry and act fussy? Of course, it was the latter, and, with some frequency, your parents came and met your need.

A similar scenario of attempting to get your needs met often plays out when you become frustrated with your partner. Now, however, you have words to cause the kind of alarm in your partner that you hope will result in him or her wanting to meet your need. Although all-too-common, this behavior pattern isn't really effective. An attempt to coerce your partner to be who you need him or her to be only leads to more negativity.

This cycle can be interrupted by creating an atmosphere of five times more positive interactions than negative. To understand why this works, you need to know that the human brain is built to be negative. Yep! Our ancestors were constantly scanning the environment to see what was possibly wrong with the picture. Is that a snake or a stick? Is that red berry a good source of food or a fatal snack?

Recent research has confirmed that the brain hangs on like Velcro to negative experiences and lets go like Teflon of positive experiences (Hanson and Mendius, 2009). This *negativity* bias is troublesome in a marriage, because your brain will naturally dwell on bad experiences and dismiss neutral or positive ones. For example, you will remember the 10 days this month that your spouse left her handbag in the middle of the kitchen table but forget the 21 days she put it away. The brain's negativity bias-survival function is necessary, and there's really no getting rid of it.

Interestingly, though, Dr. Gottman found that couples who expressed and behaved positivity with a 5:1 ratio reported feeling happy in their relationship. That is, it takes five positive experiences to balance out the negative one! So, if you routinely express positive sentiments, appreciations, and loving gestures, you will build resilience—and the one out of five times you complain or criticize will not damage your marriage. In short, the relationship savings account you have created will tide you over during spats of negativity.

Granted, everyone makes mistakes at times; inevitably, you will lose your cool, say something mean, and make your partner feel unsafe at some point in your relationship. So how do you reestablish safety once you have been negative? Take these three steps to bring back safety and connection:

- First, take ownership for your negative behavior by acknowledging you were negative.

- Then listen to understand your partner's feelings about your negative treatment.

- Then restate the situation as an "I message." (e.g., "I am frustrated because . . . ")

This also is the time for self-reflection. Perhaps you were being negative in an indirect way to tell your partner you are hurt or need something. Obviously, your negativity wasn't the right way to go about communicating your hurt or need, and you will need to apologize without justifying your behavior. After hearing how your partner felt about your treatment of him or her, you may want to request time to set aside to use the dialogue process we will describe in Key #4 in order to address what you have been feeling.

In reality, if you remember to keep the 5:1 ratio going and you turn things around when you slip and have been negative, you will be giving 100% to improving the atmosphere of your relationship. No marriage is perfect; all marriages are works in progress—*progress* being the key word.

Negativity Leaves the Door of Your Relationship Ajar

Perhaps the most compelling impact of negativity on your relationship is that it can leave your relationship susceptible to both affairs and divorce. With a history of negativity in a relationship, both parties begin to feel badly about themselves and despair about the chances of ever being happy with the other. What happens is that you both feel unloved, disrespected, hurt, and misunderstood—and this causes one or both of you to feel disconnected. Ultimately, this gap between you eases the way for a new person to walk in and replace the connection meant for your partner. In fact, chronic negativity often leaves partners with the idea that a better relationship exists somewhere else. Time spent chatting with a person at work or at the gym suddenly feels better than going home to the painful chasm between you, and you find yourself standing on the slippery slope of forming a new intimate alliance.

Regardless of whether emotional or physical, affairs are always destructive. That you are putting your relationship at risk can be difficult to admit when the flattery, flirting, and attention of a new person makes you feel so much better than all the negativity you have to deal with at home—but the feeling is an illusion! Remember that infatuation makes us chemically unable to see each other's faults, so of course, you'll find your new relationship perfect and have no complaints. This won't last, but all that matters in the moment is someone thinks you're great, whereas at home you're a disappointment.

Even if you manage to avoid emotional or physical affairs, negativity is still the major factor in divorce. As evidence, let's look closely at the two significant spikes in the divorce rate: at 5 to 7 years, and at 10 to 15 years. In those couples divorcing at the 5 to 7-year mark, "conflict" is the stated cause. When couples describe conflict, however, what they are really talking about is negativity. The habits of speaking harshly, complaining, criticizing, blaming, shaming, ignoring, stonewalling, showing contempt, and threatening the other are what "conflict" is all about.

At the 10- to 15-year mark, divorcing couples state they are disconnected and have no feeling of intimacy left. In decades of couples counseling, we have heard hundreds of discouraged people state, "I love my spouse, but I am not *in love* with my spouse." What they are describing is the lack of intimate connection that was whittled away by years of negative interactions. Intimacy and connection require safety. Negativity destroys it.

The Origins of Negative Behaviors

All feelings are generated by thoughts. All behavior is driven by feelings. If you want to treat your partner in a positive manner, you will need to *think* about your partner in a positive light. We want to teach you to reduce your negative thoughts by *observing what you think* and reframing your spin on things before you act in ways that rupture your connection; various mental techniques, challenging as well as simple, can rewire your brain toward acceptance, love, and intimacy.

First, let's look at the formula of how thoughts ultimately affect behavior:

Thoughts ➜ Feelings ➜ Behavior ➜ Reaction from Your Partner

All people walk around with thoughts in their minds all day long. In fact, researchers found that we have about 70,000 thoughts per day and that about 90% of the thoughts are exactly what we thought yesterday (UCLA Laboratory of Neuro Imaging, 2008). At the core of our thoughts is a part of the brain we could name "The Interpreter." As we go through the day experiencing many events, big and small, The Interpreter decides what those events mean, how important they are, and if they are good or bad. We call this "the story we tell ourselves"—and, make no mistake, you are telling yourself a story all day. Sometimes the story is right, accurate, and/ or fair. Sometimes the story is old and outdated, based on a misunder-standing or just your habitual viewpoint. In other words, The Interpreter often isn't right in its interpretations. If you find your thoughts filled with judgments and criticisms of your partner, then the story you are telling yourself is negative.

Because feelings follow thoughts, you will find that you feel upset with your partner much of the time if your thoughts are filled with negative interpretations. Once you feel painful feelings such as frustration, anger, hurt, sadness, irritation, or loneliness, you will begin to behave according to those feelings. Your behavior based on this pain will be to show your partner you are upset by either raining out your emotions upon them or by reining in your affection and communication from them.

On the other hand, when you find yourself thinking positive, flattering, and empathic thoughts about your partner (such as when you were blinded by romance), you feel love, tenderness, affection, and gratitude—and you will behave accordingly. When you hold your partner in a positive light, you will feel empathic and positive feelings. How might you act differently if you believed these thoughts? The power of empathy creates safety and connects you. It is the antidote to negativity.

A typical example of how the negative stories we tell ourselves interfere with relationships can be found in the self-talk of Annie as she goes through the house straightening up. Annie picks up a sports magazine left in the bathroom and tells herself, "Jeff never puts anything away. He probably thinks I just exist to clean up after him. He doesn't appreciate how hard I work all week, and he can't even thank me for my efforts. He doesn't care about me. He's always off in Jeff Land."

As Annie gets on a roll with these negative thoughts, she starts feeling angry and hurt. The more she feels angry, the more she looks for evidence of Jeff's shortcomings, and, because Jeff is human, she can generate quite a list. Never mind that Jeff is waiting in line for an oil change for Annie's car, and, after the car is ready, he is stopping on the way home to fill the propane tank and go to the hardware store for a new water filter. However, let's not be too hard on Annie. She is not the only one guilty of ongoing negative self-talk. Jeff does it, too. (We all engage in negative self-talk at some time or another!) In line at the service department, Jeff finds himself wondering why he is always the one who remembers the need to service Annie's car.

It would be bad enough if Annie were just doing her chores with a sour attitude and stopped at the negative thoughts and feelings. Like the rest of us, however, the sourness spills over into negative behaviors as well. Back to the scenario above, Jeff finally returns home. Annie has become quite angry and hurt and has had time to perfect her thoughts of blame. Because thoughts lead to feelings, her blaming thoughts cause her to feel angry and hurt. Because feelings lead to behaviors, instead of giving Jeff a hug and saying hello, Annie huffs out of the room. When Jeff follows her to tell her about his frustrations at the big box hardware store, she interrupts him and criticizes him for taking too long on his errands. She attacks him for leaving messes, for a lack of follow through, and for not knowing anything about being an adult. Ouch.

Partners are only human. As noted above, when attacked or in danger, we become defensive and go into flight, fight, or freeze. Jeff, who is a "turtle type," reacts by shutting down and retreating into *his* shell, refusing to answer Annie. Then his negative thinking takes off! Behind his fortress,

Jeff is building up a case about her shrill behavior by thinking, "She always reacts like a crazy woman. She doesn't see a thing I do. I've had it. She can change the damn filter herself!"

So, Jeff throws down the water filter on the kitchen counter and walks out to the driveway. But does it stop there? No! Annie follows him, making exaggerated statements such as, "There you go! Run away like you always do!" At this, the "turtle" snaps, and Jeff starts dumping his frustrations on her as well. "Why don't you ever take your car and have it serviced?" he yells. "What kind of adult ignores that she needs an oil change?" Back and forth with blame and criticism they go, until what could have been a perfectly good Saturday afternoon and evening is completely ruined. Because the blowup was so great, days went by before they could repair the damages.

Part of what got in the way for Jeff and Annie was that they forgot that each of them is a unique individual, different from each other. Annie expected Jeff to value the same things she did—and to show appreciation in the ways she wanted. Jeff, on the other hand, was off in his own world doing his own thing, thinking he was being a good partner by taking care of some of their chores. He expected Annie to appreciate what he was doing as well.

The point is: We often unintentionally abuse one another with negativity to change each other into our "twin," our picture of an ideal mate. But, recall, as we discussed in the first chapter, that real love and a rock solid relationship are built on seeing that your partner has a different point of view and accepting that view as equally valid as your own. Your way is not *the* way. Your way is not the *right* way. Your way is not the only way. It is just *your* way.

When you love someone, you must stop using negativity to change him or her. Accepting your partner's differences comes from a willingness to learn how to ask for what you need without becoming negative. The truth about partnership is that companionability, not compatibility, makes for a happy and romantic relationship. Companionability is the wonderful energy between two accepting partners who respect and appreciate one another.

Because there is no need to be alike, companions enjoy their differences and find that those differences are what keep their relationship interesting. Over time, you learn to rejoice in your partner's happiness as much as you enjoy getting your own way. Good companions care about seeing that their partner is happy and feels respected. Good companions make certain that each partner's interests are valued and that both points of view are incorporated into the marriage's blueprint in the areas of intimacy, parenting, finances, chores, and leisure time. When you can treat one another as treasured companions, there will be plentiful growth and change—and you will have a rock solid relationship.

Breaking the Negative Response Cycle

Given just how potent negativity is, how can you reduce the urge to act on negative thoughts and feelings and increase your closeness as companions? By training your brain to experience and convey positive thoughts and feelings!

Proactively thinking the best of your partner means listening to your negative self-talk as it occurs and replacing automatic negative thoughts with positive or neutral thoughts. If you realize you are spending too many of your 70,000 daily thoughts on negative judgments toward your partner, you will need to develop a new habit. Consider establishing the habit below.

#1: Observe your running mental commentary. Is the story you tell yourself filled with judgments, blame, and criticisms? You aren't perfect, so why must your partner be perfect? Listen to your self-talk and ask yourself, "Are these thoughts balanced and include my own shortcomings? Am I just tired, hungry or upset about something else? Am I on the offensive?"

#2: Check in on how these thoughts are making you feel. Are you getting angry, hurt, sad, scared, or lonely? *Thoughts lead to feelings in about five seconds*, so, by the time you observe your negative mind chatter, you are well on your way to feeling badly!

#3: Ask yourself, "How am I beginning to act because of these negative thoughts? Am I getting snappy, harsh, cold, sarcastic, caustic, or withdrawn? How do I think I am coming across right now?" Perhaps you yell at your partner or shut down and refuse to talk. How does your partner react when you engage in these negative actions? What reaction do you get when you roll your eyes, sigh, or look away?

#4: Consider this question: "What else can I tell myself right now that is balanced, realistic, empathic, or generous? What other explanation for my partner's behavior will help me to feel love and connection? Is my story the only story that can be true? What do I imagine it feels like to be in my partner's shoes?" All these questions lead to an increase in empathy for your partner. Empathy is the process of considering how your partner is doing, what he or she may be feeling or experiencing—and the process allows you to let go of your negative views.

#5: If there is something that is still bothering you, how can you express your negative feelings in a way that keeps you connected and helps your partner to feel safe enough to hear you? The answer to this is to use an "I message." "I messages" tell your partner about you and the behavior that frustrates you, rather than attacking them personally.

Let's walk Annie and Jeff through a "re-do," something we all must master in order to have rock solid relationships:

Annie is straightening up and comes across a magazine that didn't make it back to the bedside table where it belongs. Because she notices she is starting to feel angry, she checks on her thoughts and catches herself beginning to "make Jeff wrong" for leaving things in the wrong place. Instead, she makes a different choice and tells herself, "It's not that big a deal. Jeff lives here, too. I can put it away or leave it here and eventually he will put it away."

A little later, Annie sees that the kitchen is messy and needs cleaning before they go out later for a run. When Annie feels her growing irritation, she notices her thoughts: "Jeff is always off in Jeff Land not noticing what needs to be done." Once she recognizes the mounting tide of negative thoughts, she makes a choice to stop mentally picking on Jeff. She replaces the negatives with a fuller picture. Annie reminds herself, "Jeff is off running errands on a busy Saturday. He is getting my oil changed and then has to go to that huge home store and wander around looking for a filter. Poor guy! I know how much he hates that huge store with no help available. Jeff does his part."

Annie begins to feel better but has a hard time shaking off feelings of disappointment. She is sad that every weekend they do chores and rarely take time to camp, play outdoors, go to a movie, or have friends over for a game night. She is tempted to start making it all about Jeff's work ethic, but she catches herself and takes the time to formulate her frustration so she won't be making it Jeff's fault.

When Jeff gets home, Annie first asks him how the errands went. (He had frustrations, too.) Then she asked him if he wanted to go for a run and afterward have a talk about how they spend the weekends. Jeff responds by doing his part to put away any of his usual objections to talking through issues and makes certain to clear the way to having a conversation. Annie carefully chooses her words to use "I messages" and to make requests, not complaints. She also takes the time to give Jeff "an appreciation," *the very thing she wants,* for his contributions to their relationship. In this scenario, Annie and Jeff treat one another with empathy and respect.

Changing behavior that is so thoroughly engrained in you may seem difficult, but the results far outweigh the effort. You will experience what we call "real love." Real love is based on affection and respect. Real love is actually seeing the person you love, versus magnifying his or her flaws and minimizing his or her attributes.

To proactively reduce negativity in your relationship requires changing your negative mind chatter and being willing to hold your partner in the best light. This change requires that you think positive thoughts and spend quite a few of your 70,000 daily thoughts admiring, appreciating, acknowledging, and affirming. It also requires you to spend very few of those thoughts admonishing.

Here's a simple exercise you can use that will help you to strengthen your companionship. Whenever you think or express negativity to your partner, think of three positives about your partner and express them to him or her. This will help you to become more appreciative and hold your partner in positive regard.

Rewiring for Love

In addition to reframing negative thoughts and challenging your Interpreter to cut your partner some slack, to move from negativity to real love you will need to build new neuro-pathways of positive thoughts. When the brain is amply filled with good thoughts and associations about your partner, you will find that you *automatically* think the best of him or her.

Let's explore some *preventative* measures you can take to rewire your brain away from judgment and distance and toward acceptance and fondness. You have learned that unconscious processes largely govern your brain. That is why we need to change what is in our unconscious in order to prevent so many negative thoughts from getting started. We need to take over the controls of our brain for a few minutes each day, so that we can rewire our brain for love.

Some people are exceptionally happy in their marriages because they have what relationship scientists call "positive illusions." A positive illusion is simply a strong positive picture of a partner that overlooks imperfections. Think of the illusions created in a magic trick. A master magician draws your attention to something compelling so you don't notice the mechanics of a trick. Likewise, positive illusions allow your attention to be focused on the positive aspects of your partner, not the flaws. This is different from denial in that you aren't ignoring serious or destructive behaviors. It merely involves overlooking normal human imperfections in appearance and performance.

Norene remembers sitting with an elderly couple who had been married for over 60 years. They were seeking her help with deciding if it was time to move to an assisted living facility. She asked the husband to tell her something he appreciated about his wife. Without missing a beat, the elderly gentleman said, "She is as sexy as the day I married her."

Besides being touched by his comment, Norene couldn't help but think it was an example of a positive illusion. Sitting in front of her was a woman with gray curly hair, a thick waist, wrinkles, sagging arms, and a tee shirt reading, "World's Best Grandma." But her husband wasn't just being kind. He clearly found her as beautiful as the day they met in college. No matter where they were going to spend the last chapter, he believed to the bottom of his heart he was spending it with the sexiest person in the world. Wouldn't that be a great way to view one another as you faced old age together?

Another way to think of positive illusions is as a well-ingrained set of positive images about your partner. Because the brain's default is to the negativity bias, we must work to create the competing neuro-pathways of a positivity bias. When you dwell on what you love and appreciate versus your judgments, you will begin to feel in love once again. You will look forward to seeing one another. You will feel warm inside when you think about your partner during the day. You will feel less depressed. You will have a more fulfilling connection.

Two exercises to rewire your brain for positivity toward your mate:

Exercise 1:

For the next 21 days, two times per day, sit back and close your eyes for about 90 seconds. Do this daily whether you feel like it or not. For the first 30 seconds, release your tension by clearing your mind, breathing deeply inward, and sighing as you exhale.

For the next 60 seconds, bring into your mind a very positive picture of your partner. Maybe it is how good he looks when he has on that special blue shirt. Maybe it is how pretty she is when she is laughing. If you have a hard time visualizing, take a nice picture of your partner and look at it for a minute to conjure up happy memories.

If you do this every day for the next 21 days, you will be surprised with the far-reaching results. Because you are rewiring your brain with positive thoughts about your partner, the images will evoke positive feelings in you, which will cause you to behave in positive ways. Although your partner is possibly unaware of your efforts to rewire your brain, notice if you begin to receive more positive responses in return. This is an example of how one person can improve the tenor of the entire relationship. You don't have to wait for your partner to change before you change. If you decide to accept this challenge for the next 21 days, your partner will almost automatically respond to you in positive ways.

Exercise 2:

Once a week for the next eight weeks, write your partner a love letter. Use some of the following sentence stems to help you to get started and come up with your own:

Some of the many things I appreciate about you are . . .

- What I love about you physically is . . .
- What I love about us as a couple is . . .
- How you really touched my heart is . . .
- An endearing quality about you is . . .
- What I find sexy about you is . . .
- What I dream about with you is . . .
- When I'm alone and thinking of you, what I think about you is . . .
- What I treasure about you is . . .
- What I treasure about our relationship is . . .
- A fun time I would like to have with you would be . . .

Write a love letter weekly. Choose a regular time and put it on your calendar. We encourage you to write it out in by hand, even if you type it first. This is because the effort to concentrate on creating prose and writing it down will help to rewire your brain toward positive images of your partner. The process will help develop your positivity bias. Give your partner the letter each week. You can write it in a card or on stationery. You can mail it or leave it on their pillow.

Catch Your Partner "Doing Things Right"

We are big fans of saying, "Thank you." We thank our partners for many things. For the past 35 years, Norene has been thanking her husband for providing health insurance. Tim thanks his wife for the thoughtfulness she shows in making lunch for him. Of course, we recognize the big contributions, too, and comment upon them. Commenting on the smaller things that we might take for granted makes the atmosphere of positivity more comprehensive. Regular expressions of gratitude leave our partners with smiles on their faces and increased good will.

To create an atmosphere of positivity that nurtures your partner's self-esteem and makes him or her feel safe, seen, and loved requires taking the time to "catch your partner doing things right." Sometimes couples feel reluctant to show appreciation for the things their partner "should do." We ask you, "Why shouldn't we all be thanked for our contributions, whether they are necessary or not?" Maybe someone *should* change the sheets, but, if your partner is the one actually doing it, that is worth noticing. Your partner chose to make you the beneficiary of all of his or her hard work, thoughtfulness, and attributes. That's pretty amazing and worthy of comment. Whether one or both of you instigate the ritual of daily thanks, the environment you live in and raise your children in will be infused with optimism and gratitude.

So why is gratitude important? A significant benefit of focusing on your partner's positive contributions is that any blue mood that permeates your marriage will disappear. Research shows that gratitude cures depression. After years of conflict, marriages can become depressed and need a "treatment" regime. Just as depressed people benefit from regular thoughts of gratitude, depressed relationships need daily expressions of gratitude in order to maintain a light and optimistic mood.

The science behind thoughts of gratitude causing a reduction in depression lies in the neuroscience of rewiring the brain. When you point out your partner's valuable contribution, it makes your partner feel good. More importantly, *you* feel better because you are emphasizing the positive state of your environment. When you are seeing what is good about your life, your stress will lessen.

Conclusion

Our natural negativity bias can create some significant problems in how we look at and treat our partner. Think of your negativity as a reactive impulse that stems from what your brain was designed to do. When you indulge in this impulse and act out in a negative manner, you may feel some immediate relief from frustration, but, soon after, you feel worse. This is because being negative releases stress hormones into *your* bloodstream. The more negative you are, the worse you feel. This causes you to think and act negatively again. It's a vicious cycle, and the only way out is to do the work of rewiring your brain to have a positive bias toward your partner. Doing the above exercises will help you to develop a *positivity bias.* Over time, you will begin to feel safe, connected, and passionate again. Then your impulses toward your partner will be to compliment, soothe, touch, play, and make love.

Breaking the habits of negativity takes time and practice. We guarantee you will stumble, because we all do. We are all perfectly imperfect, and the fact that you are reading this book shows you are open to improvement. That is a very good quality. Remember our definition of *resilience*— returning your relationship to its "original shape after it has been pulled, stretched, pressed, and bent." To assure your marriage has strong resiliency keep your relationship savings account full. A big part of that is keeping the negativity out.

Lasting change comes from taking small steps, done consistently over time. A balanced game plan for change consists of working to improve your outlook and to repair any damage done when you slip up. Set an intention to be more positive, and embrace your humanness by accepting that your negativity bias will sometimes trip you up. When it does, use your tools to stop the damage. Apologize for your part, offer an appreciation to your partner (even if it's just for putting up with you), and ask to sit down and dialogue through the issue. (The next chapter will walk you through the best dialogue process we know.)

Practice these tools and, one day down the road, you will realize a long time has passed since you had a negative thought, feeling, or reaction toward your partner. You will feel in love again, passion will be restored, and your connection will be rock solid.

Reflection

What do you see about your own negativity bias? How frequently do you have a negative running commentary about your spouse?

Is it difficult for you to "catch your partner doing it right?" Are you at ease giving compliments and appreciations? What are your childhood memories about such things?

For one month, keep a daily journal of your thoughts about your partner. Are they balanced, negative, or positive? For each negative thought, substitute a neutral or positive thought. For example, if you wrote, "He never greets me when he gets home," you could replace this thought with, "He doesn't always remember to greet me when he gets home. Because I want him to greet me, in order to make a connection, I could greet him and give him a hug. Then I wouldn't be sitting here testing him to see if he greets me."

Key #4

Communication is Key,
So Dial Up the Dialogue

"It's not what you talk about, it's how."

—Harville Hendrix, PhD

Learning to have a safe conversation can do wonders for putting romance back into your relationship. Couples use their words, their tone, and their body language to convey feelings, thoughts, needs—and chemistry. If your communication is warm, respectful, and open, you will feel closer and sexier. If your communication is non-existent or troubled, you are missing out on the opportunity to make your relationship rock solid. When you begin to talk about issues you have been trying to avoid, modifying the behaviors that detract from your relationship will become easier. In fact, nothing may be as valuable to a relationship as good communication.

According to Dr. John Gottman, the famous marriage research expert, the number one factor determining if couples succeed or fail is how they resolve conflict (Gottman, 2015). Whether surprised by the arguments that pop up during early marriage or in a standoff from years of avoiding certain topics and distancing from each other, all couples struggle with conflict. Yes, that's right: Happy couples have conflicts, too. But how can they be happy if they disagree and argue? Happy couples do not expect each partner to agree with every perspective. Happy couples have mastered some means of discussing their differences without becoming negative or hurtful. Happy couples learn to resolve conflict respectfully and quickly by using some form of the following:

1. When triggered and beginning to become reactive, take a deep breath.

2. If calm enough, state the frustration using an "I" message: "When you_____, I feel_____.

3. If still reactive and falling into a bad communication habit, STOP!!!

4. Take "recovery time" by going for a walk, folding the laundry, or engaging in some other activity that will help you calm down.

5. Ask to have a heart-felt conversation and start with the sentence stem: "When you_____, I felt_____.

6. If your reactivity is too much to get yourself calmed down within an hour, tell your partner when you think you will be available to talk in a calm, courteous way. Do not leave your partner "hanging," as this will start your old pattern of bad communication habits. Your partner will not feel safe, and more conflict and distance will be the result.

The more you work to make it safe for your partner by learning good communication skills, as suggested in the rest of this chapter, the easier it will be for both of you to connect and resolve conflict. Good communication will become a cornerstone for your growing resilience, joy, and passion.

Turn Conflict Into Connection

It's a fact of life: You and your partner won't always think or feel the same about any given topic or issue. Thinking differently about money, children, in-laws, sex, or how to spend time is the norm—even in happy marriages. Unfortunately, many couples think their conflicts are because they have different viewpoints. But how you each deal with your differing styles and viewpoints is *really* the source of your conflict. Too often, couples allow their different points of view to lead to quarrels about who is right and who is wrong. Whether the topic is big or small, important or unimport-ant, anyone can begin to feel uncomfortable and threatened when his or her partner doesn't agree. Once the discomfort arises, it's far too easy to criticize, blame, raise your voice, bully, use put-downs, or deflect with sarcasm. The conflict can even make you think you are with the wrong person. Because negativity can become a vicious cycle, we get stuck in a negative downward spiral until we throw up our hands in despair.

Unfortunately, it is all too common for couples to criticize and blame each other for starting a conflict or for using a poor communication habit. We can much more easily see our partner's negative behavior and excuse our own defensive reaction. Think: How many times have you said, "I wouldn't have gotten angry if you wouldn't have…," or "You started it" or "I've told you over and over, but you won't listen." Unconsciously, we are expressing the sentiments of our "five-year-old self." That is, when we were five, we would have handled a frustrating situation by claiming, "I wouldn't have hit my brother if he hadn't teased me first!" We teach five-year-old children they must control their own behavior even if provoked, but we forget that simple kindergarten rule in the heat of conflict!

What are we really fighting about? Why do we devolve into immature and inefficient reactions so easily? Consider the wedding phrase, "And the two shall become one." Because of the desire to be understood and connected, partners confuse disagreement with danger. Remember we discussed this in other chapters? All relationships begin with the *illusion* that we are completely alike and see everything in the same way. Of course, that is a misconception. In fact, in a recent worldwide study, researchers found that 80% of couples do not agree with each other's politics (Northrup, Schwartz and Witte, 2012). Partners regularly disagree over the use of money, how to parent, how much time to spend with extended families and when and where to retire. It is completely normal and universal that partners have unique viewpoints on most matters. Nonetheless, each partner wants the other to see the issue from his or her point of view, so each will pull out protective behaviors to coerce the other to agree. When a partner's brain detects this kind of manipulation, he or she will react with his or her own self-justifying behavior. This is how negative patterns become established. Because negative patterns are unconscious, couples find it difficult to take corrective action to resolve the conflict. So negative patterns lead to more defensiveness and conflict. Left to become the norm in the relationship, the negativity pushes couples toward an invisible divorce; they begin to live in two separate worlds.

But there's hope. Negative patterns do not have to rule your relationship. Differences don't have to be a relationship breaker. Seeing things differently can be an amazing opportunity to become great partners and companions. Remember, you are in a relationship with another person who is not you! To replace conflict with connection, you need to learn new ways to communicate that will significantly lower your reactivity and defensiveness. By learning how to establish a safe conversation that leads to feeling connected, you can increase your ability to avoid conflict. You also can quickly resolve and accept differences before reverting to your old ways of talking to each other.

Our Poor Communication Baggage

As we grew up, all of us received many childhood messages. Our parents communicated with each other in front of us, and we absorbed both the good and the bad ways they interacted. They also communicated with us as we developed, and we learned what their tone, word choices, and body language meant. Most likely, they led us to believe that some feelings were okay to express and others were taboo. Maybe culture played a role in the messages we received, or perhaps some of the messages were rooted in gender bias such as "boys shouldn't cry" or "girls should be nice."

When under stress, our parents and siblings (in fact, all the influential people in our lives) probably communicated poorly. They most likely fought, got defensive, pouted, withdrew, attacked, blamed, avoided, intellectualized, denied, and displayed other poor behaviors. In a way, they couldn't help it—and neither can you. Communicating under stress is a flaw of human brain structure; the system that communicates and the system that reacts to a perceived threat do not "talk" to one another. In fact, even if you take communication courses, become a therapist, or take a marriage workshop, when threatened, you will, at times, forget your new communication tools and revert to what you learned as a kid. Your baggage goes with you through life, and it is all "carry on." You can't check any of it!

What you can do is begin to recognize the difference between your old, unskilled reactions and how you would respond if you were intentional with your response and kept a cool head. If you acknowledge the difference, you may be more willing and able to catch yourself when the recorded messages play out. You will be quicker to apologize or ask for a "redo." Also, once you understand that you communicate similarly to the people who raised you, admitting your poor behavior and being intentional about changing it will be easier.

Because how you learned to communicate your needs as an adult has a lot to do with your childhood, the place to begin to change your behavior is by discovering what *you* brought in *your* baggage. As noted in the last chapter, some common poor communication habits are criticism, blame, interrupting, complaining, case building, making demands, stonewalling, and contempt. As noted, when you resort to these behaviors, your partner will feel put down and most likely react defensively in return. Which of these poor communication behaviors do you use?

- **Criticism:** The act of judging or finding fault in your partner
- **Blame:** To hold you partner as largely at fault about something; having the attitude of "a pound of blame and an ounce of responsibility"
- **Interrupting:** To stop or hinder by breaking in when your partner is speaking
- **Complaining:** To express unhappiness, describe symptoms, and protest
- **Stonewalling:** The purposeful emotional withdrawal from your partner; often done in order to punish
- **Avoidance:** Shutting down and withdrawing out of confusion, frustration, or fear
- **Case Building:** The use of several criticisms to prove the guilt of a partner; ramping up your emotions by thinking of all the evidence of your partner's shortcomings
- **Demands:** To assert your authority over your partner and/or claim what's due to you

- **Contempt:** Statements that come from a relative position of superiority or of declaring someone wrong or guilty

- **Sarcasm:** A cutting or contemptuous remark

- **Nonverbal Habits:** Rolling the eyes, glaring, crossing arms and legs, turning away or avoiding eye contact can convey contempt, stonewalling, defensiveness, disgust and anger

Discover Your Feelings and Needs—
and Up the Odds Your Partner Will Listen

Author Earnie Larsen, in *Stage II Recovery: Life Beyond Addiction* (2009), notes that these six skills are needed for good adult communication:

1. To know what you feel

2. To say what you feel without attack or blame

3. To make it safe for your partner to say what he or she feels

4. To know what you need

5. To say what you need without attack or blame

6. To make it safe for your partner to say what he or she needs

Having these Six Skills for Successful Communication is something that doesn't come naturally or automatically to many of us. Actually, our childhood "baggage" completely controls two areas of communication: saying what we feel and asking for what we need. Any deficiency in the area of talking about what we feel and what we need stems from what we learned as kids. If we didn't learn Larsen's six communication skills in childhood, for example, then they are missing from our adult toolbox and we may need help to learn new communication tools to be able to transform conflict into connection.

Consider feelings. Although feelings are wired in us, many of us don't have an extensive vocabulary to describe them and, thus, have difficulty acknowledging and understanding what we really feel. For example, did you know that mad, sad, glad, shame, hurt, and scared are the six basic feelings and that all others are derived from them? Also, did you know that feelings aren't thoughts? They are emotions. By habit, many of us say things such as "I feel like you're wrong," or "I feel like it shouldn't be this way." Those are opinions and thoughts, not emotions.

In addition to not being able to identify your feelings, you also may not be in touch with them. Science recently has shown that many male brains are wired such that the emotional area and the language skill area have less connecting pathways than those of the average female. Thus, additional work may be needed for males to develop the connections and learn to put a name to felt experiences. Partners can help by being patient and not taking personally this challenge in describing emotions.

Here are a few exercises to help you identify your feelings

First, find a quiet place where you will not be disturbed. Let your mind go back to a positive memory of your partner during your courtship. Try to make the memory as detailed as you can. Write or journal about that memory, focusing your awareness on how you feel about the memory. You might consider the following words to try to identify your feelings: relaxed, joyful, happy, excited, thrilled, tickled, content, or pleased. List the feelings you recall.

Next, think of a time when you and your partner had a conflict. Again, think of as much detail as you can. Become aware of your feelings for this memory. Did you feel sad, angry, hurt, scared, embarrassed, or abandoned? Write down the feelings you recall.

Now practice expressing feelings appropriately to your partner. Think of something about your partner for which you have been grateful or something your partner did or said that you have appreciated. Identify the feelings you experienced when your partner behaves this way. Next, ask your partner if he or she will listen as you share your gratitude. Do this at least one time a day for a week. Then use self-reflection time to think about how you felt doing this exercise. Writing about this exercise in a journal can be helpful. Consider: Was the exercise difficult to do? Did it get easier? What did you notice in your partner's response over time?

At another time, think of a small irritation. Then ask your partner to listen as you practice expressing your feelings appropriately. Try using this format to talk about a difficult feeling:

"When you _____(state your experience), I felt _____."
Here's an example: "When you were late, I felt anxious and irritated." Do this twice more on different days within a week. Then use self-reflection time to notice how you felt. Journal about the exercise. Was it difficult to do? Did it get easier? What was your partner's response? Did you find expressing your feelings in this manner helpful and connecting?

Just as our feelings were wired in us through childhood experiences, we also received unconscious messages about our needs. All humans have what is called "normal human needfulness"; we need things from others through all stages of the life cycle. If you received negative messages about your needs while growing up, then you probably feel uncomfortable or ashamed of your needs and are reluctant to admit you need anything.

You also observed dynamics between your parents concerning needs. You saw how they went about getting their needs met. Maybe you witnessed examples of fighting about needs, or denying needs, or being a martyr. You may feel so conflicted about getting what you need that you expect your partner to be a mind reader and meet your desires without your having to ask. But this never works. Adults need much from their partners. If you don't know how to ask constructively, you will demand or criticize out of an unconscious and misguided attempt to get your needs met. If you entered adult life unaware of what you need or unwilling or unable to ask for what you need, you will resort to poor communication.

The use of poor communication habits is really an attempt to get your needs meet. It's just ineffective. Poor communication habits will only result in defensive reactions, conflict, and disconnection between you and your partner. If continued over years, the pattern of negativity will bring more distance in your relationship, because you will inevitably avoid topics that elicit conflict. The predictable outcome of this type of behavior is a loss of the intimacy that brings you joy with your partner.

Again, there's hope! You can learn to identify what you need and how to ask for your needs to be met in an appropriate manner. Here's a partial list of Normal Human Needs:

- *Availability*
- *Consistent Warmth*
- *Attunement*
- *Protection*
- *Boundaries*
- *Freedom to Explore*
- *Acceptance*
- *Understanding*
- *Attention*
- *Competence*
- *Praise*
- *Acknowledgement*
- *Values*
- *Consistent and Reliable Affirmation*

As you read this list and reflect on your childhood, which needs got met? Which needs didn't? Was one particular need is missing? Are any of these unmet needs similar to complaints that you, as an adult, have about your current relationship?

Carrying unfinished childhood issues into our adult lives is not uncommon. Here's an example of this phenomenon: As a child, Mary didn't receive validation for doing tasks well; her parents jumped in and did them for her. When Mary's parents interfered too quickly, it left her believing that they saw her as incompetent and slow. Now, when her partner, Rachel, takes a screwdriver from Mary's hands and fixes a loose doorknob, Mary becomes overly upset, automatically assuming that Rachel doesn't see her as competent. Angry, Mary abruptly leaves the room in a huff. If Mary had never experienced this frustration in childhood and had received ample affirmations for being clever and capable, it might not bother her that Rachel occasionally takes over. But, because of "unfinished business" lurking under the surface, Mary is an adult who is over reactive about a small unpleasantness. If Mary isn't able to discover what is at the root of her being upset, she will continue to make some erroneous assumptions regarding Rachel's actions.

Erroneous *assumptions* are built from the negative stories you tell yourself about your partner's motivations. In other words, the brain is constantly trying to make sense of the events that surround us. When your partner does something that upsets you, you can bet there is a negative assumption about his or her behavior. Maybe the story says: "He isn't going to listen to me," "She thinks I can't do anything right," or "I can't tell her how I feel." All of us have negative stories we project onto others, particularly our partners. These automatic negative thoughts are more about the house we grew up in than the one we live in now.

What is your story? How does it stop you from asking for your needs to be met? Is there a more positive story you could tell yourself that would help you to ask for a particular need to be met? For example, you might think, "It's okay to have needs," or "I know my partner loves me and wants to meet my needs."

When we aren't clear about what we need and what we feel, we are all guilty of resorting to poor communication habits. Also, you may have asked your partner for what you need repeatedly and now feel discouraged at the process. If this is the case, think hard about the situation. Upon self-examination, did you invariably find that you fell back on poor communication habits such as criticizing, blaming, or shaming to get your need met? By now, we are sure you know the expected outcome!

The only way to get a new result is to use a new tactic. Asking for what you need may be more complicated than saying what you feel, but a similar structure can be used. The next time you have a minor frustration, try this approach: "Are you available to listen to a request I have?" "When you _____, I felt _____, and the story I told myself about you is_____. I know you probably didn't mean it that way, but I wish you would _____instead."

Let's revisit our home maintenance example cited above and let Mary try using the better format: "When you took the screwdriver from me and tightened the doorknob, I felt hurt, and the story I told myself is that you don't think I can fix things. I know you probably didn't mean it that way, but I wish you would ask me first if I need help."

When you are ready to try this with your partner, find a time where the two of you can focus on your relationship. Do not do this when either of you is leaving or coming home, or when you are dealing with getting the kids to eat dinner. We also don't advise practicing this approach when you have had an argument. To increase the odds of success, ask your partner to use the Intentional Dialogue process described below.

Intentional Dialogue: A Tool for Effective Communication

The best communication tool we know is Intentional Dialogue as described in the book, *Getting the Love You Want*, and as taught through Imago relationship therapy and workshops. When couples learn to successfully use this process, conflict dissolves—and safety and connection can be reestablished.

According to Imago founders Dr. Harville Hendrix and Helen LaKelly Hunt, the Intentional Dialogue process involves a "sender" and a "receiver." The sender speaks about his or her thoughts and feelings, and the receiver listens without interruption or response. As the sender talks, the receiver "mirrors" what the sender said and checks to see if he/she heard the sender correctly. Mirroring is the simple art of repeating what the sender said verbatim or very close to the exact words. It is not paraphrasing or responding. The sender said what he/she wanted to say, and the receiver needs to put aside his/her own reactions or spin in order to hear what was really "sent."

Mirroring is important, because people flourish when they feel heard. As children, we all needed our parents to look in our eyes while we told our stories, to nod in acknowledgement when we shared something personal, and not to interfere with our viewpoint. As adults, we are all still hungry for this rich experience. Think back to when you and your partner were dating. You effortlessly and unconsciously mirrored each other in your words and in your body language. This happened because mirroring behaviors are attachment behaviors. They make humans feel safe, bonded, and connected.

In addition to mirroring, another important aspect of the Intentional Dialogue process is the timing. A couple's dialogue might begin with the request, "I would like to have a dialogue. Is this a good time?" If you are too angry to listen without contempt, mockery, or frustration, then wait until you have calmed down. If your partner indicates that a cooling off period is necessary, allow him or her to do so without pressure. Also, when you sit down for a dialogue, always sit across from one another, eye-to-eye and knee-to-knee, and bring your best intentions. In fact, Hendrix and Hunt recommend always starting your dialogue with sharing appreciations—and to mirror the appreciations, too!

Here is the Intentional Dialogue process in a nutshell: Either the initiator chooses the dialogue topic or issue—or you both mutually decide on one. Once the topic is chosen, the first sender states his or her thoughts and feelings without blaming or attacking. The receiver then mirrors the words of the sender. To facilitate this, the sender should pause every few sentences, so the receiver can mirror. If the sender says more than the receiver can remember, the receiver should politely raise a hand to pause the sender, so the statement can be mirrored. You both have to know the pause signal, so it won't be taken wrong. You need to be confident neither of you is stopping the other out of frustration but out of a desire to correctly capture what each is saying.

After you mirror a segment, the receiver then asks, "Did I get it all?" The sender then either says, "Yes," "Most of it, but let me say the rest again," or, "Not quite, so let me say it differently." This process continues until the sender indicates there is no more to clarify. When the sender is finished, the receiver summarizes the "send." A summary is meant to be concise. If it were written, the summary would be no more than a paragraph.

In the beginning, we suggest you limit each complete turn to no more than 10-15 minutes. This will help the receiver remember the bulk of what is said. While the receiver summarizes, the sender is quiet and doesn't interject. When finished, the receiver asks, "Is that a good summary?" If the sender needs to say a little more or clarify a point, now is the time to do it. But only add a little more. If you were finished and the receiver worked hard to capture all you were saying, don't start your turn all over again. Also, only talk about one topic during a dialogue. *This process is meant to take you deeper, not wider.* Don't segue into another complaint or issue.

Once the sender has agreed that the summary is correct, the receiver will validate what the sender has said. Validation does not equal agreement. Validation equals understanding. It is a verbal means of expressing to your partner that his or her point of view is as valid as your own. It is best to keep your validation simple. The more you say when you validate, the more you run the risk of making it about you, rather than about your partner. The perfect validation is, "What you said made sense to me." Never say, "You make sense, but I don't agree with you." That is like offering someone a chair and then pulling it out from under him/her as he/she sits. Instead, stretch into your partner's reality while you listen. Your partner is allowing you into his/her psyche and is feeling vulnerable. Don't take the responsibility lightly. Instead, challenge yourself to listen with open ears and an open heart.

Speaking of open ears and heart, the most frequently asked question when we teach couples Intentional Dialogue is, "But what if it doesn't make sense?" The simple answer is, "Then you weren't listening to your partner; you were listening to yourself." When receiving, if you put aside your own agenda, your preconceived notions, and your need to be right, then your partner's thoughts and feelings will always make sense. Remember that you married someone who has his or her own opinions and views. Respect one another by honoring and even appreciating those differences—which once were very attractive and brought you together! They may lead to relationship challenges now, but differences also make you grow more whole as you learn from and balance one another.

The final step in the Intentional Dialogue is an expression of empathy on the part of the receiver. Empathy is standing in another's shoes and imaging what feelings came up for your partner during the experience they have just described. Just as validation helps us to know that we are deeply understood in the mind of the receiver, empathy shows us that we are deeply understood in the heart of the receiver. After you have validated, share your empathy by saying, "What I imagine you feel about this is..." and insert what you imagine he or she might feel. Keep it just to "feeling" words. "I imagine you feel sad," not "I imagine you feel sad because of X, Y, or Z." Again, the more you say about the other's feelings, the more the dialogue becomes about you. Afterward, check with the sender to see if the imagined feelings are accurate. At this time, the sender is free to confirm and also to add other feelings but must take care to stay focused only on the clarification of emotion and not reopen the dialogue.

When the receiver has mirrored, summarized, validated, and given empathy, then the receiver gets a turn to respond. The receiver starts by saying, "I would like to respond. Are you ready to hear me?" The roles then reverse, with the sender becoming the receiver and using the same method of listening. Stay on the same topic initiated by the first speaker. Respond to what was said, adding your own thoughts and feelings on the subject. Steer away from defensiveness. You may see things differently, but that doesn't mean either of you is right or wrong. You have equally valid viewpoints. When you have both had a turn, you may be finished, or the first sender may want to respond to what was said by the second sender.

A nice way to end a dialogue is to take turns sharing the following: "One thing I want to remember from this conversation is..." or "One thing I want to do differently is..." If possible, follow the dialogue with having some fun. Doing something light hearted or romantic after an in-depth conversation reinforces the fact that you are friends, lovers, companions, and teammates. Consider having a dialogue once a week so you can master the process. Also, attending a *Getting the Love You Want* workshop, doing a few Imago therapy sessions, or watching a demonstration of the Intentional Dialogue on YouTube will help you to improve your skills.

The Intentional Dialogue process is deceptively simple. At first glance, it may seem tedious, corny, or flimsy, but don't be too quick to judge. It is actually a complex tool that involves several parts of the brain and requires some effort for mastery. When you are upset, the most primitive part of your brain—known as your reptilian brain or "survival central"—is activated. This causes you to go into fight or flight or to hide, freeze, or play dead. Needless to say, this reaction doesn't lead to your clearest thinking or best responses. When you dialogue, however, your reptilian brain is soothed and your brain's higher functioning centers are activated. When you mirror, you will automatically begin to breathe slower and pay attention to what your partner is saying. The process of listening in order to repeat back the words will distract you from stress and fear. Instead, you will feel relaxed, curious, and compassionate. In essence, the effort of mirroring causes you move away from basic survival and back into your heart. When the speaking partner takes care to choose words that don't incite fear or defensiveness, your accurate mirroring acts to soothe and calm your partner. This then creates a positive response cycle between you two.

As you make a habit of using Intentional Dialogue, you will discover new insights about your own behavior. With practice, Intentional Dialogue helps you to understand how your behavior contributes to the conflict, and to talk and respond in a way that increases the emotional safety between you and your partner. Over time, a new, more conscious connection with your partner will emerge. The empathy you feel toward each other will be the antidote to the old defenses you turned to when conflict arose. You will not be so easily triggered into conflict, and your relationship will become more resilient. Granted, you will still have conflict from time to time, but your ability to have safe conversations will lead you back to connection every time.

Conclusion

All couples, happy and unhappy, have conflict. The difference between the two is using a skillset of successful communication to turn conflict into relationship growth.

But communication skills usually are lacking! How your parents communicated with each other and with your siblings—and how they related to you—became your learning center. Your brain unconsciously picked up all the nuances of your family's way of interacting. If you didn't experience the six skills for good communication, then you will use poor communication habits in an attempt to get your needs met. Your partner also will have poor communication habits that will contribute to your relationship conflicts and defensive patterns.

Most conflicts are the result of misguided attempts to get your needs met. You weren't raised to give voice to your feelings and needs. You were raised, usually unintentionally, to use strategies. Some of us learned to make a fuss and protest, to cry or yell or act out in some manner. We were trying to elicit a response, good or bad. Others took the strategy of being seen and not heard. Withdrawing to stay under the radar made us feel safer than asking for something we needed. These old strategies may have worked well enough in your childhood, but your marital happiness requires adult skills for an adult interaction.

Learning the Intentional Dialogue and developing your Six Skills for Successful Communication will bring you and your partner closer and provide a foundation for making your relationship the priority in your lives. Communicating successfully is easier than you think and is worth the time it takes for mastery. Ideally, you will both work together to develop your skills, but the power of one of you making the changes necessary cannot be overstated. Whether together or alone, start today identifying your problematic communication habits and practicing these magical skills.

Reflection

Who most influenced you growing up? What messages about feelings and needs did this person/these people ingrain in you?

Think about a common source of conflict for you and your partner. What behavior or habit does your partner have that causes frustration? When he or she engages in this behavior, what do you feel? What is the story you tell yourself? How do you negatively behave in return? What childhood memory comes up for you? What could you do differently the next time it happens?

How in touch are you with your feelings? How easily do you share your feelings with your partner?

What needs do you have that aren't being met? How might you communicate those needs to your partner?

Does your behavior change when you're under stress? Do you have strategies you use to keep your cool under pressure? If not, what might work for you?

What are your poor communication habits? What triggers the reactivity?

Reflect upon Larsen's "Six Skills for Successful Communication" and how well you use each one. Set goals for improvement.

Ask your partner to try the Intentional Dialogue. Pick an issue that isn't too difficult, in order to practice without being too upset. Write down your reflection of how it went and what you would like to improve upon next time.

Key #5

Build a Firewall to Protect Your Relationship

"No one stores valuable treasures in open unsafe places.
Valuables are stored in secure environments—
away from thieves and perilous conditions.
And that's just common sense considering
the high price paid.
Out of naïvety, ignorance, or independent/prideful spirit,
some of us leave our highest treasure—
our marriage—out in the open.
Exposed to strange elements,
vulnerable, unguarded, unsafe."

—Ngina Otiend

Another hallmark of rock solid relationships is strong boundaries. What do you think when you hear the word *boundary*? Some may think, "It's about time we had some boundaries!" Read: "My husband spends way too much time with his buddies" or "My wife spends too way much time getting advice from her sister!" Others may think: "Why do we need boundaries?" "It's too controlling," or "I give my partner the same freedom to do what she/he wants as she/he gives me!"

Many couples have difficulty acknowledging how a lack of boundaries can infringe on their relationship and cause damage. In fact, for your marriage to be rock solid, two specific boundaries must be in place: confidentiality regarding the private matters of your marriage and exclusivity in intimacy (both physical and emotional). Other, less obvious boundaries are needed in order to preserve your "couple-ness." They include the agreements and practices that help you to make your relationship your top priority.

Part 1

Why Set Up the Firewall

"Having a great marriage isn't rocket science. It's simply a choice."

— Kristine Carlson

An intimate relationship is both strong and vulnerable at the same time. Think about computers. They are powerful, brilliant machines capable of teaching us just about anything and of working at the speed of light, but they also are vulnerable to viral "invasions." If a virus ever has infected your computer, you understand how quickly this strong technology can fall apart. But, because we value protecting our passwords, emails, finances, photos, browsing history, and documents, we willingly spend money for subscriptions to firewalls.

Well, your marriage is a significant investment, too! It's filled with private experiences, explicit content, memories, history, financial and legal issues, and perhaps a parenting partnership. But, like a computer, your marriage also is vulnerable to invasion. To keep it rock solid, you need a good firewall.

No matter how emotionally committed you are to your partner, the strength of your marriage will be diminished without a set of healthy boundaries. These boundaries serve as the firewall, the set of values and agreements you have to care for each other and to protect the relationship.

Setting up a firewall around your partnership is the opposite of what the cultural norm tells us to do—which is to value autonomy above everything else. That is, instead of a relationship based on, "If it's good for me, it should be good for you" or "You do your thing, I'll do mine," a strong marriage is based on asking, "What does my relationship need from me?" and "What would keep my partner safe?" The simple fact is, other people and choices you make can intrude on the sanctity of your relationship and pose a danger. Just like "good fences make good neighbors," good boundaries keep marriages safe.

Boundaries provide you with the "container" in which your profound sense of safety allows for the development of a close and healthy life-long bond. In this chapter, we will explore the various people and issues that impact the ability of couples to establish and keep boundaries. They include confidentiality, infidelity, children, friendships, in-laws, and extended families. Then we will show you how boundaries keep your relationship safe and fulfilling. Lastly, we will offer you some tips and tools for repairing the damage from a lack of healthy boundaries and/or boundary violations—so you can build your rock solid relationship and make your love last.

The "Over-sharing" Generation: What Happened to Confidentiality?

Confidentiality between partners was once a given. Although men and women may have joked or complained about their spouses, there once existed a cultural norm of "what happens in the bedroom (emotionally and physically) is no one else's business." In current times, much of this has changed. It is no longer uncommon to hear men and women share many of their marital, sexual, and personal problems with friends, relatives, their children, and even the public via social media. You may wonder, "What's the problem with a little venting?"

The problems in sharing your woes outside your relationship are extensive and serious. When you married, you committed to supporting, admiring, protecting, advancing, and growing with your partner. You committed to having his or her back! When you share your marriage's challenges and confidences, you are breaking these commitments. Doing so disables the relationship's firewalls and leaves the marriage vulnerable to breakdown and breakup.

Breaking relationship confidentiality crosses an intimate boundary. Even if your marriage doesn't suffer a fatality, this behavior can lead to feelings of hurt and betrayal. When you blame, judge, or criticize your spouse with others, you are allowing the listener into the sanctity of your marriage—and you are imposing your viewpoint on private matters. Venting private details about your spouse or your marital struggles to others, even an individual therapist, is rife with problems. Each time you rehash "your side of the story," you simply reinforce your belief that your partner is all to blame. This leads you to feeling worse about the relationship and less accountable for your contribution. Remember your negativity bias?

This biased venting causes your confidants to develop a negative opinion of your spouse. People you share with will seldom call you on your part of the dynamics. Why should they? There you are complaining about someone who isn't present and probably taking little responsibility for your part in the problem. What about this scene would make the listener feel safe to call you to task? It is simply too intimidating.

A particularly sticky area of venting occurs with adult (even younger) children. If your romantic relationship has become distant over the years, letting your children become your closest allies and sharing confidences with them about your marriage can happen too easily. If you share in this manner with your children, however, you are eroding their respect for your spouse—their parent—and, ultimately, for you. It is crossing an important parent-to-child boundary; you are not supposed to make your children your confidants! It is essential for you, and for the development of your children, that you and your partner share the closest bond, with everyone else outside that intimate circle.

Sadly, sharing with friends, relations, or colleagues often surpasses or replaces the emotional intimacy that should be unique to a couple. If you turn to your friends or relatives to vent about your unhappiness instead of speaking directly and responsibly to your partner, you could be paving the way to the end of your relationship. When you turn to someone outside your marriage, you are creating an unhealthy dynamic of collusion. You have forged a secret alliance about your spouse's shortcomings. This is an alliance in which, behind your partner's back, you have been saying intimate, personal, and unflattering things to an outsider.

Consider: Is your venting in keeping with your commitment to your spouse that you will love and honor him or her? Can you imagine how you would feel to find out he or she is doing the same? Even if you think your spouse will never find out you have been sharing critical comments, it is very likely that, in the midst of a heated fight, you will blurt out, "And my mother (best friend, sister/brother, therapist, our daughter) thinks you are wrong, too!"

We aren't suggesting you keep "confidences" about abuse in your relationship. If you are suffering from physical, sexual, or emotional abuse, it's vital you seek outside help. But venting isn't usually about abuse. It's about making the spouse look bad and reassuring yourself you aren't to blame. Except in situations where abuse exists, that is never the case; we are each 50% responsible for the dynamics between us.

Having "leaky" boundaries is usually a misguided attempt to resolve frustration. That any of us feels stymied about how to solve the chronic issues in a marriage is understandable, and that we would turn to others for help makes sense. The problem is, venting to others doesn't help and only makes matters worse. Sure, venting may offer temporary relief, but you didn't talk to the one person who could truly improve things: your partner! This misstep derives from our fears of conflict. All of us have memories of conflict going very wrong. Because we never learned to engage in conflict constructively, we unconsciously avoid it.

If you want to be a good partner, you must learn how to have a healthy dialogue to resolve conflict as well as to embrace the role of one who admires, advocates for, acknowledges, affirms, and appreciates your spouse. If you do talk to a confidant, represent your partner in a positive or neutral light, and take responsibility for *your* shortcomings. Not only will you gain the respect of the listener, but you also will signal to him or her that you are open to feedback about *you*—because only *that* feedback can result in positive change!

Part 2

Boundaries Can Prevent Affairs

"Throw your heart over the fence and the rest will follow."

— Paul Newman

With a divorce rate of 51% and a sexual infidelity rate of 21% of men and nearly 15% of women (National Opinion Research Center, 2010), it's obvious that many couples are struggling with infidelity and insecurity in their marriages. The affair statistics may appear lower than you imagined, but they do not include "emotional affairs" which are thought to be just as destructive. Because affairs are less about a lack of love and more about a gradual slide across boundaries, taking boundary setting seriously is crucial. That is, if you want to have a happy, relaxed, secure, and committed relationship, a love that lasts, then you need to understand the boundaries you must put in place and respect in order to keep your relationship rock solid.

One of the most prevalent myths about affairs is that they happen because there is something wrong with your marriage. What we know now is that affairs happen in happy marriages as well as conflict-filled marriages, and that many conflict-filled marriages never suffer an affair (Glass, 2004). Nonetheless, nearly all affairs start with innocent behaviors. For example, you cross boundaries of emotional intimacy when you share with a "special friend" intimate information you would normally only tell your husband or wife. At that point, you open a window to let in the affair partner—and erect a wall between you and your spouse.

When you share personally with another you bond with that person. Self-disclosure is the principle way in which people become close. When you chose to share personal stories and details with someone outside your marriage, of the opposite sex, or of the same sex if you are gay, you are choosing to create a gap in the firewall that protects fidelity. It is a choice, not an accident.

In many marriages, people spend far more time at work and with their colleagues than they do with their partner, so it's not surprising that 40-60% of affairs start at work (Glass, 2004). The workplace offers endless opportunities for the gradual slide from "friend at work" to emotional affair partner. Teamwork, travel, projects, and longer work hours all lead to a growing closeness between two people who share common interests. At some point, colleagues might even realize they are sharing more at work than they are at home. Eventually, this ample time spent side-by-side sharing emotional excitement creates an emotional intimacy.

Affairs that begin at work don't necessarily arouse your partner's suspicions. After all, you must be at work in order to provide for the family. Texts and emails that come from a colleague wave few red flags, because legitimate business may be discussed. In fact, when the slide into an affair happens with someone from work, acknowledging the affair yourself might be challenging. Your own denial may keep you from seeing that your feelings are growing into something more.

The same susceptibility that occurs in the workplace can occur in many other arenas. Time spent solo at the gym, school and sports activities with your children, and college classes and professional clubs are all opportunities and places to get to know others on your own. In these situations and at these places, you may meet someone who could be a new friend, but, if you are honest with yourself, you could see how spending time alone with someone and getting to know him or her can be a risk for a married person. This type of friendship is exactly the kind that opens an emotional window to allow a new person to move from friend to affair partner. At home, you hear about troubles with children, bills, tasks to be done, finances, and dissatisfactions. The budding affair partner offers someone who can relate to your daily grind and offer empathy without bringing any of the stress that home involves. He or she might seem to understand you better than your real partner, and this makes him or her much more attractive.

As with a work affair, as the closeness increases over time within any of the above scenarios, being honest with yourself about the nature of the relationship can be tough. People having emotional affairs are often in denial about their potential to ruin their marriages. But *any* secretive relationship that opens a window of intimacy with an outsider and erects a wall between you and your partner is destructive—and a betrayal. Once the window is open, the intimate feelings with the "new friend" can easily slide into an affair; the quick hug good-bye turns to a lingering hug and then to a kiss. In fact, affairs that start out slowly and build a connection before progressing to sex are often the most difficult to break off—and the most damaging to the marriage.

E-motional Affairs

A lack of boundaries on social media also can lead to affairs. The term "e-motional affairs" describes the upsurge in Facebook users starting an innocent friendship that ultimately destroys their marriage. After all, breaking your partner's confidences and sharing your deepest feelings is much easier when someone isn't sitting right across from you. You'll feel more comfortable taking risks you wouldn't take in person. Real life (and your real relationship) may begin to feel stifling. Soon you may feel as though your online friend knows you better than your partner. Although an artificial sense of intimacy, this idea can begin to consume your thought—and seem all the more exciting because it's a secret.

Social media also makes it far too easy to reconnect with past romantic partners and start up where you left off. If you had sexual contact in the past, recalling how it felt and even romanticizing it as being hotter than it was in reality is tempting. But old flames are in the past for a reason. Most likely, that reason is you ran into the relationship challenge phase, and one of you ran out the door.

Seeking out an old flame is not an innocent behavior but puts you on the edge of a very slippery slope. Marriage counselors' offices are full of people who started out with an online search for an old love interest—for whom they are now leaving their partner.

The only safe way to have outside friendships (online or in person) is by being 100% honest and transparent with your partner. If you especially enjoy the company of someone of the opposite sex—or, if you are gay or lesbian, of the same gender—that "friend" needs to meet your partner. Having no secrets is one of the secrets of a rock solid relationship!

One way to "try out" a healthy outside friendship is to invite the colleague or new friend to lunch or dinner with you and your partner. If your partner has a bad feeling after meeting your friend, then you must stop seeing that friend alone. And you must stop communicating with that person about anything other than necessary business via phone, text, and emails. This may sound strict, but it is nonetheless wise.

If you have friendships that could already be emotional affairs or could lead to an emotional affair, ask yourself the following questions:

- *Do you find yourself sharing deep thoughts and feelings with someone you find attractive? Do you discuss details and problems about your marriage?*

- *Would you not want your spouse to hear what you are saying?*

- *Do you feel romantic excitement about someone outside your marriage?*

- *Do you lie to or keep details of your life from your spouse?*

- *Do you get dressed up for someone in order to draw his or her attention?*

- *Do you hide your cell phone messages, texts, or emails from your spouse?*

If you answered "yes" to *any* of the questions, you are putting your marriage at risk. Get help from a marriage counselor now. He or she can help you to stop the affair in its tracks and to make your marriage happier and more fulfilling. If you realize an affair is already under way, you must stop it immediately. You have entered the infatuation stage with a new person, and your partner cannot compete. If you are uncertain you want to continue your marriage, go to a marriage counselor anyway. He or she can help you to discern if there would be value in attempting to improve your marriage before you give up completely. Many couples have succeeded in reinventing their relationships after an affair. Falling for someone new can be a real wake-up call and can be the point at which a couple decides to reinvest in their marriage and bring it to greater life. Obviously, the refreshed marriage will have stronger boundaries, but what occurs within the boundaries will be more gratifying for both partners.

Part 3

Protecting Your Relationship from the Demands of Children and Family

"Our lives and circumstances will not automatically line up to support and celebrate our marriage vows. It's our job to make sure they do."

—Ngina Otiende

Having children is a game changer in romantic relationships. Perhaps most significantly, you must divide your energy, and there's less of you to go around! In our counseling offices, many couples muse about going back to the time, before they had children, when they had the luxury of devoting time and attention to one another. It's not that they don't want the kids; in fact, they would die for them. But they miss the closeness and intimacy they once felt—and still need in order to feel happy and secure.

As we discussed in previous chapters, finding time for your relationship can be challenging when added to your other demands such as work, chores, and tasks such as paying the bills. But having children is like no other stressor and is far harder to contain within boundaries. A chronic problem in troubled marriages stems from allowing the children to cross the boundaries that should give your relationship the time and energy needed to maintain your connection.

The Boundary Challenges with Newborns

Remember the saying, "two's company and three's a crowd"? The birth of a child is no easy transition. Most couples have difficultly finding adequate time for their relationship when the baby arrives—and someone gets left out. With the first baby, you shift from being madly in love with each other to being madly in love with the new resident of the household.

When once you only had eyes for each other, now you only have eyes (and hands, breasts, and kisses) for the baby.

Most likely, the person who feels left out is Dad. While Mom is nursing the baby, the bonding hormone of oxytocin is being released, causing her to feel content. Because cuddling with Dad just isn't as wonderful, some men complain they are competing with the baby for their partner's attention and affection.

Another area of concern during this phase of parenting is the "family bed." Because mothers usually experience exhaustion when the baby is very young and needy, moms usually need help so they can rest. A common strategy to alleviate this issue is sleeping with the baby between Mom and Dad on the bed—or having Dad sleep on the floor. The family bed is a legitimate and bonding child-rearing style, but couples must recognize the unique challenges of getting enough sleep *and* enough intimacy when children are present during the night.

Granted, the needs of the newborn do supersede the needs of your relationship in order for secure attachment, but the baby's needs require *flexible* boundaries. Working together to find time for your relationship will take a variety of *creative* interactions. Plan for small daily deposits (a hug, kiss, gazing glance, an appreciation), find time for intimacy and sex, and have an occasional date night (without the baby). The second and third suggestions may take careful planning, and, yes, even more sacrifice—but they will keep your connection alive during this early child-rearing time.

Unfortunately, couples frequently tell us they don't have enough "me time" to exercise, read, and get a little extra rest. This may be true, but "me time" can't come at the expense of "we time." During your child's infancy, you must triage and make your infant the first priority, your marriage the second priority, your needs for personal time the third priority, and house-work the fourth priority. You can have an Intentional Dialogue, as outlined earlier in the book, each Sunday evening after you put the baby to sleep and look at the week ahead in order to plan for those priorities.

Chores and a clean house can come later in life! So many parents stress over cleaning and cooking, yet, years down the road, you most likely won't wish you had spent more time doing chores. You might wish, however, you had spent more time parenting together, playing on the floor with your baby, sleeping an extra 30 minutes, or having a glass of wine and watching TV or a movie together.

As with any issue, we suggest using the Intentional Dialogue to explore both of your ideas for maintaining your relationship, the household, and your sanity. Never is there a time in your marriage that sharing your expectations is more necessary. Just as you might make a list of the chores that need to be done during the week ahead, make a list of how you are going to have daily intimacy, family time, and alone time. Daily actions such as foot rubs, sharing the highs and lows of the day, and bathing the baby together will go a long way toward maintaining your connection. Weekly plans to schedule sex at naptime, a date night out of the house, or a family trip to the zoo will help you to have things to look forward to. Monthly, you might consider arranging a romantic and sexy evening at home or an overnight trip to the beach for the whole family. Whatever you schedule, do your best to stick to it. The negative pattern that leads to relationship trouble starts when couples do not find time for one another during early child rearing. This early time sets a precedent for your family life to come.

The Difficulties of Boundaries with 3-18 Year Olds

Boundaries are necessary in order to protect, nourish, and maintain your marital connection. Consider this example of a typical homecoming in which an important boundary is neglected:

Imagine coming home from work, and your sweet little child is excited to see you. He races for you, calling your name and begging to be picked up. You need to hear about his day. You need to see what he made at school. You need to play with him. You try to stop and acknowledge your partner, but your child pulls you away. You can't have a conversation alone with your partner, because your child doesn't want to be left out. By the time you read Junior a bedtime story and get him to bed, it's late and all you want to do is go to sleep.

The boundary that is neglected in the above scenario is the connection between you and your partner. Unfortunately, placing children's needs before the needs of the relationship is all too common. Some couples don't want life to be this way; they just don't know what to do about it. Others believe that children's needs should always come first. We want to assure you: You can have securely attached, well-loved children who get the attention they need *and* a securely attached marriage in which both partners feel well loved and get what they need. Life doesn't have to be either/or. When children *always* come first, however, everyone suffers— you, your relationship with your partner, and the children.

Let's replay the homecoming scenario and use two small boundaries that would improve the evening for everyone: You come home from work, and your sweet child is excited to see you. He races for you, calling your name. You pick him up and give him a big hug. Then, putting him down, you say, "I need to say hello to Mommy (or Daddy) and give him/her a hug." If Junior is young, you might carry him on your hip and find your partner for a greeting. If Junior is old enough to play independently, you can escort him back to his play and reassure him that you will be back in a few minutes. If you are dealing with adolescents, you can redirect them to the dinner chores or homework and assure them you will return in a few minutes to check in and help. Either way, you can find your partner and "welcome" him or her with eye contact and a long embrace or greet one another with a short affirmation such as "It's good to see you" or "I missed you." Then you follow up this connection with asking, "How was your day"? Do you think a few minutes of checking in with each other would make a difference? You bet it will!

After connecting with your partner, then you can return to your child. You may even find you actually have more energy, so much so that you get your child down at the designated bedtime (another healthy boundary) and still have energy to cuddle with your sweetheart. Regular and reasonable bedtime for children is crucial to the health of your marriage. It's not easy because most kids want to stay up. But they want to ride without a car seat, they want to eat only cookies and they want new toys each day. In other words you impose many boundaries that your children have come to accept.

Hopefully, you can see where greeting and redirecting your children (first boundary) and getting them to bed on time (second boundary) protects and nourishes your relationship. We challenge you to come up with your own specific boundaries and experience the results yourself.

The Ultimate Challenge: Boundaries with Your Adult Children

Many marriages end up in crisis over adult children. Your relationship with your grown children may be very different than what you experienced with your parents. With no models of reference, you may feel you are floundering in this area. When your children were young, the expectations of how to respond to their needs were clear. When your children are grown, the roles and expectations about your obligations are far more ambiguous.

In responding to your adult children's requests and needs, you and your partner need to be a team. Establishing boundaries with adult children is vital to the health of your marriage, and your marriage's health is still vital to your children. In fact, the phenomenon of "gray divorce," divorce occurring after the age of 50, is on the increase. Today, Americans over 50 are twice as likely to divorce as they were 20 years ago (Schulte, 2014). The adult children of these divorces are just as sad, hurt, worried, and frustrated as their nine-year-old counterparts.

What are some of the challenges to your marital security posed by your relationship with your adult children? One contemporary issue is that of adult children continuing to live at home into their late 20s or 30s, or moving back home due to economic hardships or divorce. Sociologists think that multigenerational living can be very good for our society; marriage counselors agree, with cautionary warnings. At a time in life that couples assume that their nest will be empty and their time dedicated to enjoying each other's company, many couples find themselves doing extended parenting. Extended parenting can bring extended disagreements for the couple. In short, when children stay home or return home, sliding back into parenting is very easy. And, this time, the kids really don't want to be told what to do!

Your marital security demands that you two are on the same page concerning your child's financial and chore contributions as well as the inevitable lifestyle differences. Unless an adult child is quite ill or disabled, your adult children should be contributing both money and chores to your household. It is not their right to live with you past the age of 18; it is a privilege you are extending. As a couple, you need to dialogue until you reach agreements about healthy expectations. Then, together you need to present the house rules and policies to your child. What about noise? How do you feel about late-night visitors? Is it really okay with you if your child sleeps until noon? Once you share the rules with your child, you and your partner need to have each other's backs about those rules. If you allow your child to get away with breaking an agreement and your partner gets fed up, siding with your child is the opposite of protecting your relationship's boundaries.

Also, if you have fully independent adult children living in your area, you and your partner will need to decide together how often you will babysit, what vacations to which your children will be invited, if you will loan them money, if you are comfortable with them using your home and belongings, etc. It is beyond the scope of this book to spell out any healthy answers to these questions. We pose them so you will proactively discuss the issue, come out of any denial, and preserve the specialness of your relationship.

At times, the drama and chaos of an adult child can drastically challenge the boundaries of a marriage. How to best prioritize the needs of a child who is struggling with life-threatening issues such as drugs, alcohol, or mental illness—or even how to make him or her a priority—can never be crystal clear. That ambiguity, along with the fear and frustration of the situation, can cause partners to turn on one another.

We believe that, in these circumstances, setting healthy boundaries around your relationship requires additional resources other than just intention and effort. Al-Anon, the 12-Step program for families of addicts, and the National Alliance on Mental Illness, the support system for families of mentally ill children, offer books and groups to educate you on how best to survive issues that are entirely out of your hands. Warning: Do not let decisions regarding how you will each relate to your child be driven by unconscious guilt. Together you need to question how much of your need to "fix" your adult child comes from feeling responsible for how he or she turned out or the problems he or she faces.

Your child's struggles with life will ultimately bring you two closer—or create a wedge. Wanting to feel needed by your kids can be quite seductive—familiar, close, warm, and fulfilling. But the job of a parent of adult kids is to help them stop leaning on you to their (and your) detriment. Your job is to foster independence. Your marriage needs you. Your partner needs your attention, devotion, time, and resources. The bumper sticker "We are out spending our children's inheritance" may be comical, but it also speaks of a life in which the parents now have an empty nest and can enjoy the rewards of their efforts versus prolonging the commitment to consider their children's needs.

At every stage of family life, children whose parents make their relationship THE priority are more securely attached. The children of such marriages see their parents modeling a healthy relationship. They see their parents loving each other, caring for each other, and repairing any conflicts. The children of these marriages also find they can't come between their parents. This provides a safe and secure base for a happy childhood.

We often tell couples, "The best gift you can give your children is a rock solid relationship." Putting your relationship first is not about neglecting your children. It's about giving them a view of what it looks like to have a safe and passionate relationship. And it starts with maintaining healthy boundaries—with them.

The Extended (and/or Blended) Family

Unclear boundaries regarding extended and blended family—parents, in-laws, siblings, children, and stepchildren—can be another source of conflict between partners and cause marital discord. You were born or adopted into a family long before you met your partner, and you adapted to your parents' expectations when you were little. You may be fine with your parents' expectations, but your partner may not.

Your parents may expect you to spend Sunday going to church and stay-ing through dinner with them. Your in-laws may expect you to join the family business and work out of town six days a week. Your stepchildren may not allow you to parent them. Your children may not like living with you and would rather be with your ex. Your husband's brother may expect him to go fishing every weekend. Your wife's mother may refuse in-home nursing care and expect her daughter to take care of her physical needs daily. It usually isn't that any of our extended or blended family wants to be difficult. It's that they don't always think to make space for the new people or new arrangements.

Although there may be input or expectations from the extended family, these types of interactions usually become a problem only when one of you forgets that your partner must always be considered first. Too often, one partner can put his or her extended family above the other in all sorts of ways that leaves his or her partner "out in the cold."

Consider the following example: Jill and Sam continue to have ongoing conflicts about her parents. Jill's parents have always wanted her to see the world, and she grew up going to many exotic places. After she married Sam, her parents would call her with their latest plans for the next trip and had already booked tickets and motels—for them and Jill. These plans either did not include Sam, or he was informed he could go if he could buy his own tickets and pay for his own motel.

Sam and Jill couldn't afford these expenditures, so Sam couldn't go. When he complained he felt like a "second class citizen," Jill, feeling irritated, would counter: "I told you before we married that my parents like to do this with me. You said you were okay with it." Sam, now also angry, would reply, "I didn't realize these trips would take up all your vacation time and leave us with no time to go anywhere together!" This may sound drastic, but, if this couple doesn't figure out how to protect their relationship, they most probably will be in serious trouble down the line.

Here are a few actions Sam and Jill might use to support their relation-ship: First, they could save up enough money to include Sam on the next trip. Secondly, Jill might use a boundary statement with her parents such as, "We want to include Sam on the next trip I take with you. We will wait until we have saved enough money to pay his way. We appreciate that you still pay my way, but I want him with us, so we will wait until we can do that. So, please always check with me before you book anything." Another way Jill and Sam can help Jill's parents to honor the new marriage and its boundaries is to explain to the parents the importance of Jill and Sam allotting their limited resources and vacation days to trips for just the two of them. Sometimes we need to kindly remind those outside the primary relationship that the marriage is the highest priority and comes first.

Family expectations range from large to small. Jill and Sam had a large issue, but most marriages have multiple small ones. One small boundary violation might be agreeing to a request or expectation without your partner's buy-in. For example, you might say, "Yes, I will babysit" (never mind you planned to go to a club that evening to hear music with your spouse), or "Yes, we can pitch in money for Uncle Bert's fishing trip" (without checking it's OK with your partner), or "Sure, we will come to dinner Saturday" (although your wife had already made reservations for a romantic dinner for two). Unfortunately, we are often too afraid to disappoint our family members and unconsciously fall into the mindset of "I would rather beg your forgiveness over something (saying yes to a family demand) than ask your permission."

As the antidote to this dilemma, we suggest you always respond to anyone else's requests by saying, "Let me get back to you about that. I need to ask (your partner)." That boundary is the basis for postponing any agreement with another until you have had the chance to discuss the opportunity or request with your beloved.

Protecting your relationship doesn't mean you should not have a connection with extended family, but you need to set boundaries for your relationship from too much intrusion. Here is a list of questions we call "predict it and plan it" that can be used to set boundaries to protect and meet your relationship needs. Using the Intentional Dialogue process, explore the following:

Predict It:

- What is the typical situation that occurs?

- How does it make you feel?

- What do you need from your partner in order to feel supported?

- What does your partner need from you that would feel supportive?

Plan It:

- What actions can you take to be supportive?

- What action are you willing to take to be supportive?

- What actions can your partner take to help you feel supported?

- What action is your partner willing to take to support you?

This is not a dialogue to work out a compromise or a bargain that has as its baseline, "What's in it for me?" More exactly, the conversation is a tool for collaboration that takes into account both of your needs and helps you to be a team that supports your relationship.

It Takes a Village to Raise a Marriage

If you are married, you probably stood in front of your minister, family, and friends and spoke vows of honor, fidelity, love, and devotion. Why you did this goes beyond pleasing your parents and the haul of gifts that helped you to start your life together. The bottom line is, it truly takes a village to make a marriage work. After all our cautions above, we want you to know that having close relationships with those outside your marriage is extremely important and helpful.

Those of us who have long-lasting, happy marriages feel blessed to have many terrific relatives and friends who expected us to be our very best in our marriage. If we were to come to any of them and gripe about our spouse, these wonderful people would remind us that each of us is 50% of the problem. These people are our "tribe" and invaluable in keeping us on track and helping us work on our marriage. They expect us to speak well of our spouse and would defend him or her if we did not.

Your parents may be a tremendous source of support for your marriage. If they have remained married or have remarried successfully, they can offer guidance and feedback based on knowing you well. Although you should maintain your privacy, you always can ask them how they have managed to sort out things over the years. Asking questions about your own shortcomings is always okay! Your parents raised you and are aware of your personality and character challenges.

Turning to successfully married couples in your church or synagogue is another source of support for your vows. If you attend a church, a Bible study group for couples can be a tremendously useful support system for staying accountable in your marriage. Often, these types of groups go on for years, and close friendships come of them.

Likewise, groups that form around issues of parenting can help you to successfully navigate those issues. No time of life is more challenging for a marriage. This phase requires a network of friends and family that will help you to carve out the very important alone time your marriage will always need.

Sit down together and evaluate the strengths of your current relationships with family members and friends. Do they help you to be a better spouse? Are they true and faithful to their partners and speak well of them? Do they hold you personally accountable for your character flaws and imperfections? Are they sober and healthy? Do they tell you secrets about their relationships?

Be sure your friendships are with people who will help you to uphold your marriage commitment. If you already are struggling, tipping you into hopelessness won't take much prodding. On the other hand, having established true support systems will give you people to turn to for wise counsel. Making a marriage work really does take a village—and some thought has to be given to whom you welcome into your village.

Part 4

How to Repair Broken Boundaries

"It has been said that time heals all wounds.
The truth is that time does not heal anything.
It merely passes. It is what we do during the passing
of time that helps or hinders the healing process."

— Jay Marshall

Boundary breaches must be repaired. In instances both great and small, you must take steps to regain your partner's trust when you neglect or dishonor the agreements and practices that protect marriage's sanctity and safety. When you don't uphold your agreements, you need to have a conversation with your partner, "make it right," and, depending upon the seriousness, get help to prevent a recurrence.

Boundary violations can be divided into two groups: 1) actions that over time erode our boundaries and, therefore, our connection and 2) those that will quickly destroy our connection.

Boundary Crossings that Erode Connection

Eroding boundary crossings consist of breaking with the agreements you have made with your partner that were designed to keep your marriage your highest priority and those that involve agreements and decisions with other parties such as your children, your own family, and the in-laws. All committed relationships struggle with some boundary crossings. Even we authors have examples of boundary crossings in our own marriages. For example, when we decided to form a business together, we didn't first consult our spouses. We drew up and agreed to our business contract on an airplane over the Midwest! Our spouses had never met our new business partners and had no advance opportunity to raise questions about time, money, and sensibility. They weren't happy. Later, although they fully enjoyed and accepted our new alliance, that didn't justify the boundary crossing. We didn't have a written agreement to never start a business without the consent of our spouses, but the boundary violated is that of *"always tell your partner your plans and possibilities before you tell anyone else."*

Other eroding boundary violations are things such as spending more money than you agreed to spend (and then perhaps lying about it!); saying "yes" to requests for money or favors from your children, relatives, and friends before consulting your spouse; and venting about your partner to others. In most situations, the infractions themselves will not end your relationship, but, done repeatedly over time, they can ruin a perfectly good marriage.

The conflict these kinds of boundary breaches cause, combined with the resultant feelings of disregard and disrespect, leaves partners feeling hopeless they will ever be considered. Over time, the hopelessness becomes resentment, which only creates more conflict and distance that further erodes your connection. Remember, connection requires safety, and crossing the boundaries in your marriage diminishes the safety.

Just as we have, you will make mistakes in this area. Our agreements are well intended when we make them, and the emotions and unconscious agendas from which we operate will inevitably cause us to slip. Once you realize you crossed a boundary, what should you do?

1. **Admit to, or acknowledge you crossed a boundary.** "I realized today, after the fact, that I told my sister we could watch her kids this weekend before consulting you. I know that I agreed, before I give away our time, that I would check with you."

2. **Apologize.** "I'm sorry for not keeping my agreement with you. It was wrong of me."

3. **Validate.** "You are right to be upset with me. It makes sense to me that you are frustrated and disappointed when I ignore agreements I made to you, my partner."

4. **Make an attempt at insight.** Try to see why you may have either

forgotten (unlikely) or ignored (more likely) agreements to the most important person in your life. What was the story you were telling yourself at the time of the boundary crossing? What do you remember feeling? What kind of rationalization did you use? Is there something about your childhood experiences that makes it hard for you to keep certain promises? Maybe you're thinking, "I realize now that I am still afraid to tell my sister 'no.' When she acts disappointed or desperate, I feel so guilty and trapped. I know it isn't her fault that I said 'yes.' It's my own issue. But I think I'm still like a little kid with her."

5. **Make amends.** Sincerely ask your partner what he or she needs from you to make it right. Remember, you were a part of setting the boundaries in place that are designed to keep your relationship the highest priority and most precious entity. You aren't a victim of the boundaries; you benefit from the boundaries. So, be willing to fix things when you break them. For example, in relation to the above scenario, you might say, "I would be happy to call my sister and be honest with her about my mistake of not checking with you about our plans. I won't make it about you, but I will let her know she needs to find childcare because I was mistaken to agree to her request. Or, if you feel it is fine to watch the kids, I will let her know in person that I broke our agreement to check with one another first and that I hope she will help me to always remember to do so going forward."

6. **Reinforce the successes.** The times you notice you are keeping the boundaries strong deserve a mention. Pat yourself on the back when you realize that, despite temptation, you kept the boundaries. "Hey, I want you to know that Owen and Mara asked us to watch the kids next Saturday. I knew you wanted to watch the college football game, so I told them we couldn't. I feel really proud of myself that I thought of your needs this time!"

7. **Revisit your boundaries periodically.** It never hurts to check in with each other periodically to see if you are both sticking with the agreed-upon practices and policies that are the nuts and bolts of your boundaries. Some questions you might ask are:

- How are we doing on our spending plan, our parenting policies, and our setting aside special time?

- Is there need for improvement in how we interact with our in-laws?

- Are we spending too much time at the office, on the computer, or posting on Facebook?

- Are we upholding each other's confidentiality and keeping our partner's image positive with our friends and family?

- Are we keeping with the agreements about loaning our grown children money, or buying them gifts? How about our holiday spending?

Boundaries are like the buoys used for ocean swimming races. When you swim in the ocean, powerful currents pull you away from the finish line across the bay. Buoys mark the course and exist to guide the swimmers to their destination. Ocean swimmers look up frequently to see where they are in relation to the buoys, so that they can correct their course. They know the currents will pull them away from their target, and they plan for it. Boundaries can be wonderful buoys to assure our success at staying on course.

The Ultimate Boundary Crossing: Infidelity

As noted above, any inappropriate relationship involving emotional and/or physical intimacy is dangerous. Affairs are at the top of the list, but other kinds of relationships with outsiders also can be threatening. These include pornography, prostitution, sexting, strip clubs, online relationships, emails, and voicemails.

Many actions and behaviors including alcoholism and other addictions can put your relationship in peril. Infidelity, however, is the most painful and personal. You can easily view your partner's addiction as his or her own problem, but, with an affair, it's as though a bomb goes off in your relationship and the sound "relationship house" you built with your partner shatters. The foundation of your vows and agreements is gone, and it will take time and hard work to recover and restore trust. For most couples, it's difficult to imagine that the marriage can continue. Some will not survive the infidelity.

If there has been an affair in your marriage, you need to seek professional help. Repairing the damage from infidelity requires not only a structured approach but also a qualified counselor who has experience working with couples and infidelity. Couples can repair, recover, and grow with qualified help. Couples who chose the path of doing the work of infidelity repair often claim to have stronger marriages with increased communication and intimacy. These couples learn to turn a devastating situation into an opportunity to explore the deeper issues that opened the window to the affair. Couples who do not seek help struggle with ongoing mistrust, anger, despair, and punishment.

The Five Steps for Affair Repair

Consider these five steps for repairing the damage caused by an affair:

Step 1: Acknowledge the affair and make amends

Step 2: Stop the affair

Step 3: Rebuild trust

Step 4: Rebuild intimacy

Step 5: Forgive

The first step is to acknowledge the affair and make amends. This is often called the "discovery period" in which the affair comes to light either through the unfaithful partner's disclosure or the betrayed partner finding out about it. After acknowledging the affair, the unfaithful partner can begin to make amends for the deceit by answering any and all questions the betrayed partner may have about the affair. Questions the betrayed partner might want answered include: how long, when did it start, where and when did sex take place, and has it ended. This should not be a one time "Q&A." Due to the shock of discovery, the betrayed partner will likely have more questions and want more information as time goes on. The trauma for the betrayed partner produces PTSD. It will take time, empathy, and patience from the unfaithful partner to repair the deep wounds caused by the affair.

However the affair comes to light, it is common for the unfaithful partner to deny, lie, or own only a part of the infidelity during the discovery period. The main reasons for this are: he or she is not sure whether to end the affair, he or she doesn't want to hurt the spouse any further, he or she doesn't want to face the guilt and shame, or some or all of these reasons. This will only prolong the discovery period and cause further damage as the betrayed partner will experience re-wounding and think trust can never be restored. Full disclosure during the discovery period is crucial.

If you have not already ended the affair, the second step of repairing the damage from an affair is that the unfaithful partner must end it. Cold turkey! The unfaithful partner cannot "just be friends" with the other person. "Being friends" is how the affair started, and the betrayed partner will not trust the unfaithful partner to keep the relationship at a friend-ship level. All exclusive and intimate contact must be stopped. If you work with this person, you will need to create boundaries that your spouse accepts. For some couples in some situations, the unfaithful partner can establish adequate boundaries at work that include no exclusive contact and conversations limited to only necessary work topics. Depending upon the situation, some unfaithful partners have to change jobs in order for their marriage to survive.

While it may seem that the unfaithful partner deserves to be punished for his or her betrayal, understanding his or her struggle to end the affair can benefit the repair process. He or she formed an emotional attachment, and ending it creates feelings of loss. If this is not acknowledged, it can create ambivalence in his or her desire to repair the marriage. Individual counseling with a qualified professional can help the unfaithful partner process his or her grief without re-wounding the spouse.

The third step of repair is rebuilding trust. This step involves being trans-parent, accountable, and willing to create boundaries to protect the rela-tionship. The unfaithful partner can be transparent by allowing the betrayed partner access to all emails, voicemails, texts, and social media sites such as Facebook. Trust will increase when the unfaithful partner is accountable to their partner about his or her schedule and activities. Allowing your partner to check your whereabouts and informing him or her of any changes helps to repair the breach caused by the affair. Also, keeping any and all agreements you make, or immediately getting back to the betrayed partner when you cannot keep those agreements, increases trust.

A particularly sticky point in this regard is running into the affair partner. To prevent this, it pays to consciously avoid places where contact could occur. It is also wise to work together to create a plan for how each partner will deal with any inadvertent contact with the affair partner—such as when dropping off the kids at school or shopping at Costco—that might occur even with the best of avoidance attempts.

One of the most troublesome boundary crossings is when the unfaithful partner has ended the affair and the affair partner continues to make contact. Make a plan with the betrayed partner about how this will be handled. This plan should include any phone calls, text messages, voicemails, emails, or social media contact. Discuss how to handle any physical proximity with the affair partner. Tell your partner when an attempt to cross boundaries has been made by the affair partner, and how you followed the plan. Although uncomfortable, this will rebuild trust. Even though your spouse may re-experience the pain of your betrayal, he or she will feel more distrust if you don't tell him or her.

Incidental triggers in normal life events are another area that brings up the pain of an affair. Watching a movie that features an affair or having a waiter or waitress who looks like the affair partner are examples of incidental triggers. When the unfaithful partner demonstrates under-standing and empathy for such triggers, trust can be restored.

We recommend using the Intentional Dialogue process to explore specific actions you can take that will increase trust and repair the betrayal. Be mindful this will be an ongoing process that will take time and perseverance. The more the unfaithful partner takes responsibility and takes action that brings healing, the sooner the trust will be restored.

The fourth step toward repair is to rekindle intimacy. This part of repair leads to a deeper connection and more honesty in the marriage. There are two parts to this step: 1) learning from the affair and 2) rekindling intimacy. The first step is to accept that your old relationship is over. It may have been a great relationship or a terribly flawed one, but in order to move forward you must let go of what was and work with great intention to build a new one. Although affairs aren't caused by a relationship being faulty, you are faced with the task of learning new skills and repairing the firewall that was breached.

When one of you cheated, he or she decided to try to meet personal and intimate needs outside the relationship. Discovering what problems were present for the unfaithful space and why he or she made the choice to cheat, is crucial to building a new, vital, strong and honest marriage. When couples have issues that cannot be addressed successfully, those issues will go underground and create conflict, distance, or both. This can leave the couple susceptible to an affair because underlying needs for attention, affection, sex, being heard, or feeling accepted begin to get met by someone else. Many other things such as low commitment from the beginning of the marriage, the stress of raising children, working and paying the mortgage, mid-life crises, and losses in life are also common reasons individuals decide to step outside the marriage.

What is important here is to get to the bottom of the underlying reasons for the affair. Then you can meet the needs that were acted out through the affair. When couples are successful at supporting each other's needs, they move away from the toxicity of the affair to a much more connected and safe relationship. They are more honest and often create a relationship that is better than their old one. The work of getting to the underlying reasons for the affair is best done with a qualified professional; it is emotionally challenging to have a conversation that keeps both partners from being defensive so they can make sense of the affair.

The second part of rekindling intimacy is to put more physical and emotional presence into the marriage. Again, use the Intentional Dialogue process to explore ways to feel more connected. What are some small actions you would like from your partner on a daily basis? What are some activities you both could do together regularly that would increase connection? What can you do for fun? Do you have a get-away on your calendar? Make a plan and follow through.

Also, you both will benefit from increased affection. Discuss what it is that you enjoy. Holding hands when you take a walk? A kiss and a hug when you greet each other after a day's work? Cuddling on the couch while you watch a movie? Yet again, we challenge you to use the Intentional Dialogue process to explore ways you can demonstrate affection. Come up with a list and commit to do something on the list daily. You may find this difficult at first, if affection hasn't been in the marriage for quite some time. But you don't have to be perfect; you just have to make an effort. Making the effort and following through will help rekindle intimacy.

Sex is critical to rekindling intimacy as it bonds you and re-creates safety, connection, and passion—the three things all couples want in their relationship. Of course, sex can be problematic for a variety of reasons. You may have had a diminished, unsatisfying, or non-existent sex life prior to the affair. The betrayed partner may think he or she is being compared to the affair partner. Desire can run the gamut from intense sexual feelings right after the discovery of the affair to no touching or affection. After an affair, sex can become a very tricky arena full of potential triggers. If needed, seek professional help to understand each other's thoughts and feelings about sex. Artfully negotiating the pain and betrayal caused by an affair can bring a renewed sense of sexual desire that is vital to a full recovery.

Whereas both of you need to feel your partner is receptive to rekindling intimacy, it's important to note that the betrayed partner needs to be wooed and the unfaithful partner needs to be accepted for his or her attempts at initiation. The betrayed partner needs to know the unfaithful partner wants him or her and has chosen them again. Withholding sex and affection—or retaliatory behaviors such as the betrayed partner having an affair of his or her own—will decrease the chances for repair and healing.

Likewise, the unfaithful partner needs to know that his or her attempts to rekindle intimacy are helping. When the attempts are not helping, the unfaithful partner might be "overreaching" when the betrayed partner is not ready. An example would be giving too much affection when the betrayed partner is not ready to receive it. When the unfaithful partner has made unsuccessful efforts to rekindle intimacy, he or she often becomes discouraged and stops trying.

Every couple has their own pace for rekindling intimacy. Ongoing use of the Intentional Dialogue process can assist couples in sharing information that can be helpful in targeting efforts and successfully pacing the repair.

The fifth step of repair is forgiveness. When safety, trust, and connection have been restored, it is time to forgive. Forgiveness allows both partners to let go of the past, affirm the present, and embrace their future.

Lingering resentment and shame can be replaced with restored trust and respect. A renewed feeling of love can emerge. We recommend this be done using the Intentional Dialogue, so that both partners can express elements of their growth and healing.

Some couples attempt to jump right to this forgiveness step in order to put the affair behind them. When the first four steps go unaddressed, unresolved pain and issues continue to leak into the relationship and create conflict, mistrust, and distress for years to come. It is imperative, therefore, that partners work through the first four steps of affair recovery so that true forgiveness and repair can be successful.

When the unfaithful partner chooses to repair the damage caused by the infidelity, he or she will ultimately confront his or her shame. This can lead to finding it difficult to forgive his or her self. Verbalizing the shame to the betrayed partner and receiving validation and forgiveness helps the unfaithful partner to forgive him or her self.

Each affair has its own story. What the affair means to each partner and his or her marriage cannot be put into a neat, one-size-fits-all box. For some couples, the depth of betrayal, despair, and mistrust are so overwhelming that the relationship cannot be repaired. For other couples, the damage of the affair acts as the springboard for a deeper, more honest and intimate relationship. For couples who choose the path of affair recovery, their patience, perseverance, and empathy can bring real love—the kind of love at the base of a rock solid relationship.

Reflection

How well would you rate your adherence to the boundaries that keep relationships safe? Do you practice good couple's confidentiality? With whom do you leak confidences about your relationship or partner? To whom do you gripe?

How are your boundaries with your children, your family, and your friends? Do you honor "sacred couple time," or do you agree to activities that take away time you and your partner need?

Do you have a secret crush on someone outside your marriage? Are you willing to stop energizing this crush and cut off private ties with this person?

Make a list of current secrets you have from your partner regarding spending, relationships, or promises made to others. Are you willing to share this with your partner? If the answer is "no," ask yourself how keeping these secrets benefits you? How would you feel if your partner kept these same secrets?

Key #6

Keep Your Sex Life Alive

"Sex is play."

—Margo Woods

As we noted in the "Love is a Verb, So Focus on the Action" chapter, sex is one of the many actions of love that keep a relationship rock solid. It's so important that we've devoted this entire chapter to it.

Sexual intimacy is one of the few things couples share exclusively with one another; it exists only in the realm of the relationship. During the infatuation phase of your relationship, you likely felt high levels of sexual desire. Remember when you couldn't keep your hands off each other? When you couldn't get enough sex? During the infatuation stage, you had higher than usual testosterone levels that caused your sex drive to increase beyond its normal "set point"; the infatuation hormones made for an increased libido, so you were driven to forge a connection with your new love.

Once you committed to your partner, nature had accomplished her goal of bonding you to a mate in order to procreate, and so the infatuation chemicals dissipated. Heightened sexual drive was no longer needed for survival of the species, so you returned to your sexual "set point." If with that "set point" you have managed to maintain a good frequency of having sex and a mutual level of sexual satisfaction in your relationship, good job! You are insuring a greater chance at longevity in your life and your love. If you haven't, we would like to help you to understand the importance of improving sexual intimacy in your partnership.

An Ounce of Oxytocin a Day Equals a Lifetime of Love

The bottom line is: A good sex life is a hallmark of a rock solid relationship. Sexual connection serves a vital purpose and is a reasonable expectation within a committed relationship. Rather than just needing sex for reproduction, humans need sex to reinforce attachment between partners. In committing to your partner, you probably agreed upon monogamy and took him or her out of "circulation." A reasonable expectation of this agreement is to do your part to help keep your sexual life alive.

From the scientific perspective, sex is one of the main ways in which you and your partner experience heightened blood levels of oxytocin, an important chemical with multiple benefits in sexual and emotional health. This bonding hormone is nature's way of keeping us feeling close. Early in the relationship, when touch is at an all-time high, the oxytocin secreted makes us form a strong attachment. Later, our continued sexual and affectionate touch refreshes that bond.

Oxytocin occurs naturally in men and women and is thought to be critical in helping couples to succeed at living monogamously. Often called "the cuddle chemical," oxytocin makes you feel closer to one another—sexually as well as emotionally. In an interesting study, when oxytocin was administered to men via nasal spray, they experienced a 46% improvement in sexual function. Surprisingly, men who received extra oxytocin in the study even experienced an increased desire for monogamy. That is, they not only had increased sexual desire and prowess, but they also had an increased attachment for their partner and an actual repulsion for other women (Scheele, Wille *et al*, 2013).

When you and your partner cuddle, hug for 60 seconds, or caress one another, your oxytocin level goes up. The higher level leads to sexual arousal and improves sexual function. This may be why sexually resistant partners don't want to cuddle, because cuddling has the potential of leading to sex. Many partners have complained that men can't seem to cuddle without wanting sex, and this may be the reason why; increased oxytocin levels make men feel close and loving and maybe even wanting to further express that love.

If you have sexual resistance, we hope you will consider the importance of good sexual frequency for a monogamous bond. Oxytocin literally makes our partner the most appealing person to us and increases negative feelings toward outsiders. Talk about improving your chances of avoiding affairs and making your relationship rock solid! Oxytocin is designed for just this purpose.

Don't Let Life Get in the Way of Sex

Without the infatuation chemicals, we need to take over from Mother Nature the job of keeping our partner attached to us. Having sex is one of the most effective ways to accomplish this. If your sex life has dwindled, it may just be that you have developed poor intimacy habits. Perhaps nothing is "broken"; perhaps you just need to improve your habits and add a shared intention to get your sexual intimacy back on track.

Author John Gray (*Men Are from Mars, Women Are from Venus*, 2012) delightfully delineated three varieties of sex: "fast food," "home-cooked," and "gourmet." "Fast food sex" consists of those quickies focused on results. They don't involve much "lead up" but merely what gets the job done for you both. "Home-cooked sex" is longer and may be more playful and intimate. You have the leisure to savor each other. "Gourmet sex" is very special. It may include a dinner, bathing together, and maybe even a weekend away to spend a long time in bed. Happy couples feel good about all three varieties and are free to use whatever style fits their situation. Unfortunately, too many couples put sex on a back burner and allow their sexual intimacy to fizzle out.

Among the most common reasons that good sex habits diminish are busyness and stress. Once you commit to each other and the infatuation hormones dissipate, you begin the sometimes grueling work of living together—negotiating how to divide household chores; managing careers and finances; buying a home and car; and perhaps starting a family. This crazy busyness is stressful and can cause great anxiety, both of which lower your libido. But, in all honesty, busyness is most often a choice, and you can intentionally prioritize your relationship so you have time each day to connect. Also, sharing stress-reduction activities such as exercising, walks, meditation, yoga, laughter, and fun will help you both to relax and connect. Note here that we said *sharing* these activities. Done alone you will feel much better, but the stress-reduction activities may not lead to more sex.

Another very common reason sex loses momentum is because of children. Granted, your kids should be a top priority in your life, but if you aren't having a good sex life, they are at risk for living in a broken family.

Having children brings huge changes into our lives. The caring and nurturing of those little ones can be an overwhelming responsibility that leads to less sleep and less time to be intimate. Also, whereas children are a wonderful addition to our lives, raising them takes an enormous amount of energy. Many of us hope the baby sleeps through the night just so we can get rest—forget even the notion of sex! Also, for some couples, a mother nursing her baby can lead to less interest in sex; some fathers report feeling rejected and unimportant during this time. When this happens, having a dialogue free of criticism and blame is crucial; neither parent is at fault! The *situation* of rearing young children is what creates the obstacles to intimacy.

Hearing and understanding each other's feelings about what is happening—or not happening sexually—should be the focus of the partnership when children sidetrack sex. Once you feel understood, then you can strategize times for physical intimacy. Get the kids to bed early and on schedule, so you can make love. Find a sitter you can take them to, so you can have sex dates at home. Have weekly dates away from the kids, so you are more often in the mood. Sexual connection culminating in an orgasm does not have to be the goal of every sensual interlude. If you are too exhausted, cuddling, touching, and foot massages while watching a television show may be just what the doctor ordered.

Beware, too, that today's culture, in general, is at odds with maintaining a vibrant sex life. Granted, the openness surrounding sex has been healthy on many levels; for example, women have come to accept their sexual needs and desires, and men have become more interested in what makes women tick. But television, the movies, music videos, and advertising all set us up for failure and frustration by establishing the social norm of having a really, really hot love life. Could this unattainable, unrealistic cultural expectation be playing a role in the fact that couples today are actually slowing down in their sexual frequency? That's right! A British study, thought to be representative of most Western nations, shows that members of Generations X and Y are having sex on an average of 4.5 times per month. In 2004, individuals between the ages of 18-44 were having sex 6.5 times per month (University College London, 2013).

Another contributing factor to lower sexual frequency in Western nations may be the abundance of distractions readily available. Checking email, looking at your sister's vacation pictures on Instagram, or checking Facebook to see if your friends are having drinks at the new hot spot all seem to be taking precedence over reaching out to the real person next to you.

Finally, the length of your relationship may be another reason sex is lessening in priority. When you have been together for years, maybe even decades, boredom can ensue as your intimacy falls into predictable patterns. In the beginning, you and your partner experienced a great deal of novelty in your lovemaking; in addition to taking care of your desire, your greater levels of hormones also gave you courage to initiate sex and explore. In addition, as we age, our sexual appetite changes and may lead to lowered desire for physical intimacy.

But loss of sexual desire need not occur if we are game for making our sex life a priority. The trick is to be *intentional* about doing the things that keep the flame burning. Here is a place to start—a quick list of "intimacy deposits"—to help you improve your sexual intimacy habits:

- Sleep together.
- Go to bed together at least four times a week.
- Cuddle. In bed, on the couch, anywhere.
- Hug and kiss when you leave and return home.
- Put sex on your To-Do List. Make it a priority.

- Have regular date nights, hold hands, kiss in the car before you come back inside the house.

- Make the bedroom a special place—with no TV—just a place for sex and sleep. Keep it neat, so you aren't distracted. Lock out the dog and cat regularly.

- Kiss passionately every single day!

- Get enough sleep and exercise.

- Reduce your general stress so you can relax in the bedroom.

- Limit your alcohol consumption.

- Hold hands when you walk together.

- Turn off the electronics, put down your book, decline invitations to be with others—and open up more time for sex.

Planning for a sexual rendezvous can take some effort, and, yet, it is critical to the health of your relationship. Some couples are concerned that planning takes all the fun out of sex because it isn't spontaneous. But being intentional about creating time for sex actually does just the opposite. Use the knowledge that sex is scheduled to increase your anticipation. Spend some time in advance thinking about how wonderful the experience will feel. A bit of forethought can do a lot to increase your excitement. Lastly, once you are making love, does it really matter that the experience was planned? Putting sexual interludes on your calendar may help you to relax and find pleasure in knowing that you and your partner make the time for sex to be a priority.

How to Reignite Your Love Life

Monogamy requires honesty, generosity, exploration, commitment, disclosure, and scheduling on the part of a couple. Step one of mastering this list is to make certain you know how to please one another. Maybe that sounds obvious, but, in decades of couples' counseling, we have found that not all individuals have the owner's manual for their own sexuality, let alone their partner's. Sexual desire is a complicated thing arising from each person's own "Love Map."

A proven winner in moving toward more intimacy and sex is to have conversations about your sex life. If you are going to spend a lifetime together successfully, then you cannot be shy! Find a way to talk about your sexual needs and physical pleasure. What do you desire? What would increase your interest? Do you have any fantasies the two of you could act out that would fan the flame? What do you want to hear or see that would spark interest? Talking about this frankly will not obligate you to anything. Instead, it will increase trust, and as a couple you can decide what suits the two of you. Also, ask your partner what loving actions might increase his or her desire. Sometimes it isn't really an erotic action but a caring behavior. We once heard a story about how a husband mopping the kitchen floor was considered foreplay by the wife.

As you talk through your sex life, consider exploring your health and body image, as both can sometimes play a big part in sexual openness. If health and body image seem to be the culprits in your stalled sex life, two choices exist: One is that you accept your body and your partner's right now. Just stop looking for flaws in either of you. Everyone ages, lots of us put on weight, and eventually gravity will make us all sag. Stop judging and start caressing. The second choice (although you can do both) is to start exercising and eating right. Join Weight Watchers, get a trainer, go to yoga, see your doctor—do whatever it takes to look and feel your best. You owe it to one another to stay healthy. Marriage is, hopefully, for life, and you will have to take care of one another as you age. Live a healthy lifestyle, so you can do so gracefully.

We would also like to address some issues that we, as marriage counselors, encounter when dealing with women. Sadly, we regularly see women struggling with lagging sexual desire. Many feel guilty they don't experience that spark often enough, but they also feel disappointed and cheated. Why is this happening so frequently? Interestingly, for decades, women and men have suffered from the myth that intercourse will bring women to orgasm. In fact, less than 30% of women have an orgasm from intercourse alone (Medical Center for Female Sexuality; Berman, 2013). This is not a psychological issue but entirely dependent upon a woman's unique genital anatomy. If you are female and have difficulty achieving orgasm, you may want to read about techniques and sexual acts that could help make orgasm possible. Lonnie Barbach's book, *For Yourself: The Fulfillment of Female Sexuality* (2000), can help women to better understand their own sexual anatomy and needs.

It's also important to understand the "desire discrepancy" between males and females. Consider these facts: Men most often experience desire, followed by arousal, and then followed by sexual release. In contrast, women most often experience arousal, then desire, and then release. That is, for many women, desire is not the trigger for lovemaking but, rather, its result. In yet other words, women often begin sexual experiences feeling sexually neutral, but, once they engage in sensual activities—such as kissing, cuddling, and caressing—then they likely begin to feel desire as the encounter progresses. Willingness is the key. So, for women in particular, the first step of a pleasant sexual encounter can be simple willingness. This reality may be what is at the bottom of women's desire to feel emotionally connected via conversations and activities as a prelude to sexual connection. If women must first be willing to warm up to sex, they may need to feel close in order to feel receptive. Having open and honest discussions as a couple about the differing arousal cycles can go a long way toward meeting the sexual needs of each partner in a relationship.

Men are not free of sexual difficulties either. Erectile disorder, premature ejaculation and a lack of sexual desire have all become quite common. Given the cultural myths that men are always "ready, willing and able"; getting help can sometimes be embarrassing or uncomfortable. In fact, many men experience shame over any sexual trouble and are unwilling to talk to their partner or physician. There are multiple contributors to men's sexual issues including health, stress, alcohol and most recently an over dependence on pornography. If any of these issues sound familiar, the good news is that each one has successful solutions. Help can be found from your primary care doctor, your marriage counselor and even the Internet.

Unexpressed marital conflict may also be putting the skids on your sex life. If you are withholding sex to punish your partner or because you are estranged due to conflict, you need to learn skills to improve your communication. Withholding sex happens all too often and will lead to a risky disconnection. Relationships need sex in order to prevent unnecessary conflict. If you are avoiding sex because of hurts and wounds you are maintaining a vicious cycle and may need the help of a trained marriage counselor. Or attend a weekend couples' workshop to overcome the divide and get a fresh start with new tools. Good communication and good sex is a lasting combination for rock solid relationships.

Pornography: Friend or Foe?

The use of pornography as a means to explore sexuality and increase eroticism appears to be on the rise for couples (Kerner, 2011). Shaking couples out of their "bedroom boredom" by viewing pornography both separately and together seems to be gaining acceptance (Kerner, 2011). Sex therapists, educators, and advice columnists who support this viewpoint believe it can help inform and revitalize your sex life. But you need to understand the possible negative consequences in order to determine if pornography is good for your relationship. For some couples and individuals, it spells danger. With 24/7 access via the Internet, watching pornography can easily turn into sexual addiction.

In our office, we have heard women express feelings of betrayal over their partner's use of pornography. This betrayal sometimes feels as threatening as an affair. Men frequently don't understand why their viewing pornography is so bothersome. They think it has no bearing on their attraction to their wives. They may even state they are very attracted to their wives.

A partner's viewing habits may leave a woman feeling objectified, betrayed, and not able to measure up to the images their male partner finds attractive. Additionally, men may feel as though they are being compared to the males portrayed in pornography. In essence, the sexual prowess shown in pornography can make both men and women feel inadequate with their partners. Feeling attractive when your partner is using porn to become aroused with you is difficult. It is even worse when your partner loses interest in you sexually altogether. Fortunately, all of this can be reversed. Understanding the impact of pornography on your relationship is key. Does your partner feel as though he or she must compete, feel betrayed, or unattractive when you view pornography? If so, then you will have tension between you that will affect your sex life. That tension also will spill over to other areas of your relationship and create more disconnection and anxiety.

Using the Intentional Dialogue process to explore each other's thoughts and feelings when pornography is an issue can bring understanding and change to your sex life. Finding new ways, other than pornography, to bring the spark back into your sex life can revive your connection. Ending the use of pornography when it has clearly brought division between you is a loving act that shows you care about your partner. Having empathy for your partner, who is struggling to end the use of pornography, will help to encourage him or her to continue to work at abstinence.

For many of us, sex was a taboo subject when growing up, so it is often challenging for couples to talk frankly about it as adults. Hearing your partner's views about feeling connected sexually can be enlightening. By using the dialogue process to explore your desires and differences, you can discover how to create a sex life you both enjoy. Your goal should not be a race to achieve orgasm but a journey to a lifetime of pleasuring each other and achieving physical connection.

Conclusion: Great Sex Binds You Together

Everyone has a unique "sexual intimacy owner's manual." Be honest about yours by sharing openly with your partner. Using the Intentional Dialogue process can make a sexual conversation a safe experience—and bring you relief and better sexual fulfillment.

Sexual intimacy is one of the main ways you make your relationship THE priority. This doesn't happen with the act of sex alone but also in the carving out the time to enjoy one another romantically and sensually.

Having a great sex life over the course of a lifelong relationship takes intentionality and dedication. It is worth the effort, because sex is the glue that binds you close together. Sex produces hormones of patience and tolerance. Sex makes you laugh, touches you tenderly, and makes you cry in relief and love—all of which are emotions that bring connection.

Make the time in your schedule to enjoy the real living partner beside you. The physical pleasuring of one another makes your relationship even more of a treasure. Remember, sex is the one thing that really sets your relationship apart from all others. It is mysterious, special, and even sacred. Don't miss out on all that sexual intimacy has to offer.

Reflection

Are you comfortable with your own sexuality? Do you know what you need sexually and are you able to articulate your needs to your partner through either words or actions? What stops you from talking to your partner? What might be the first step for you to take to open the conversation?

Are you generous sexually with your partner? As much as possible, do you say, "yes" to his or her advances? Do you make advances of your own?

Are you actively avoiding intimacy? Do you withhold sex as a punishment, to get a point across, or out of resentment? If the answer is "yes," are you willing to talk to your partner about this?

What do you need in order to be "in the mood" for sex? What does your partner need? Have a dialogue with your partner about your responses and work on fulfilling those needs for each other, one step at a time.

Do you find you're too tired or too stressed too often to have sex? If "yes," why are you too tired or too stressed? What is going on in your life that can be altered to alleviate your overwhelm? Are you willing to make changes in your lifestyle to address your overwhelm? If "yes," what three things can you do starting today?

Talk to your partner about John Gray's three sexual varieties: fast food, home-cooked, and gourmet. How do you each feel about your sexual habits and styles? Do you want to mix it up a little more?

*Read **Mating in Captivity** by Ester Perel, or John Gray's **Mars and Venus in the Bedroom**. Talk with your partner about your discoveries.*

Key #7

Make a Practice of Regular Maintenance and Repair

---

*"We (my wife and I) have developed a practice of leaning
into the tough times…and looking at those as an opportunity
for us to get a lot more intimate,
to know a little bit more about each other."*

—Jeff Bridges

In every long-term relationship, there are predictable times when the commitment has its vulnerabilities. Whether early in the marriage when the partners are young, or later in life when the kids have caused a gap between the parents, periods of strain can cause one or both partners to become discouraged. Left unaddressed, this discouragement can escalate into despair and lead to an affair, estrangement, or divorce.

At the base of the "slippery slope" is the common dilemma of all relationships that we've already mentioned numerous times: Our partners do not think and feel the same way we do, so we can't always have our way and our needs go unmet. In our frustration we react in ways that are ruinous to relationship.

But our differences do not have to be deal breakers! The main problem in getting through the inevitable relationship challenges is that most of us don't have the knowledge and tools we need to turn toward our partner, discover what is at the source of our conflict, and deal with our differences in a proactive, positive way. When we continue over the decades of a committed relationship to work through the bumps and barricades of

normal life, we fall in love many times . . . always with the same person—
or better said, with the person we see growing right before our very eyes.

Why don't we arrive at adulthood with the tools necessary for a great
relationship? The answer is simple: We never formally learned what is
actually happening during conflict and how to manage conflict to create
a deeper connection. Think about it: We go through driver's training to
learn to drive a car and get a license. We go to school to earn a degree
or a certificate to ensure we have the skills we need for a career. But the
hardest challenge we will ever undertake—that of living with another
human being for the rest of our lives—only demands putting down
$20 to get a marriage license. No training or education required. If you
had never driven a car, would you know how to drive without training?
If you didn't receive the education and build the skills necessary for a
career, would you be successful? Probably not.

In essence, you arrived at your adult relationship with no formal training
on how to turn conflict into connection and without the information
about what to anticipate throughout the various stages and phases of love.
You also brought along baggage from your childhood about what marriage could or should look like. In fact, you may have decided early that
you didn't want a marriage similar to what you observed in childhood;
but, under the stress and strain of normal life, you saw yourself and your
partner slip into the old negative behaviors your parents modeled. Even
if you witnessed what you considered to be a wonderful marriage, your
parents' marriage skills did not automatically transfer to you. Sure, they
may have been safe drivers, too, but you still needed driver's education to
learn the mechanics of driving a car and to hone your reflexes!

Successful couples have tools to use at home to make small repairs as
needed. They also have an openness and interest in getting more advice,
help, and even intervention when the issues have become more than can
be repaired at home. We want to help you know how to do the small
repairs fast—and inspire you to overcome your resistance to getting
professional training or help fast, when it is needed.

Reasons We (Foolishly) Avoid Getting Help

Unfortunately, too many couples wait too long before they seek effective relationship help. As noted in our introduction, research shows that once troubles begin, couples wait an average of six years to seek help (John Gottman, The Gottman Institute at www.gottman.com). That means that, once a couple is in trouble, they simply fight it out or freeze each other out—for about six years! By waiting this long to get professional help, the health of the relationship has seriously declined. In fact, the relationship may even be on life support, with one or more of the partners wanting to pull the plug.

Why do couples wait so long to seek help? The number one reason people fear getting the help they need is they have a fairytale in mind that has at its core the destructive cultural myth: "If I choose the right person, we will live happily ever after." By now we hope we've convinced you this myth is quite bogus. There is no such thing as "the right person" who will, like magic, make "happily ever after" an automatic given. Every relationship is a work in progress and, to be rock solid, needs work—all the time, every day, forever.

Another reason so many couples avoid getting help is they are ashamed their relationship is in trouble. Some say they don't know anyone who got help and so it's not something they thought of, or, if they do know a couple who used a counselor, they claim the counseling didn't work and the couple broke up anyway. Too many couples also are embarrassed to admit their bad behavior. Others say having their partner in counseling with them feels too risky—that he or she might say terrible things or never own up to his or her issues. Be assured: If you get help from a certified relationship counselor, that person will know how to make both partners feel safe enough to be honest about how each contributes to the problems.

But choosing the right intervention, coach, or counselor is critical. If you need heart surgery, for example, you wouldn't see a general family practitioner; you would consult a cardiologist. Likewise, if your relationship is on "life support" and about to collapse, you must seek a certified relationship counselor. Without specialized relationship training, a counselor might not have the skills to advise you on issues specifically related to marriage. Some even advise their clients to get a divorce the very first time they meet! No counselor has a right to suggest you end your relationship. In essence, he or she is suggesting you commit "couple suicide" because your relationship is depressed! That same counselor would never suggest that a depressed individual consider suicide. If this happens to you, leave the office and don't return. Then seek help elsewhere.

Lastly, a common fear of embarking upon finding help is that it's too late. Do you think your relationship has a fatal disease and that going to a counselor will deliver the fatal blow? Cheer up! It is never too late to get the help you need. And no problem is too big to tackle.

Your At-Home Repair Kit

All rock solid relationships require learning to make repairs, both small and large, and knowing when its time to get help. If you follow our advice about making the regular deposits into your relationship savings account, you will be doing the work of maintaining the health and fitness of your marriage. However, even couples who have highly adventurous and romantic relationships still run into disagreements that escalate into conflicts. You can't expect to live with another person and always get along perfectly. Sometimes the escalation is from being too tired, too hungry, or too overwhelmed. Who doesn't have those moments?

Happiness doesn't lie in having a conflict-free relationship. Happiness lies in the willingness to repair those negative conflicts. Small repairs—any action or statement that deescalates tension—are needed on a regular basis. John Gottman found that individuals who are able to offer small repair gestures and to receive those of their partner are far less likely to divorce. Here are some suggestions of the small repairs you can start doing now when friction gets too heated:

20 Possible Repair Attempts (done with a soft tone)

1. "I would like to hear you. Can you say it more gently?"

2. "I might be taking it wrong, but that felt like an insult."

3. Open your arms to invite your spouse in to be held.

4. "Would you listen to me now and try to understand? I will then listen to you."

5. "Can we hold hands for a minute and just breathe?"

6. Can we take a break? I'm getting too worked up."

7. "Let me try again."

8. "How can I make things better?"

9. "I'm sorry. Please forgive me."

10. "I would like to tell you what makes sense to me about what you are saying."

11. Reach your hand out gently to touch your partner's hand.

12. "One thing I admire about you is . . . "

13. "I think we may be getting off track. May I summarize what I think you were saying?"

14. "You have a good point."

15. "I love you."

16. Quietly lean closer to your partner if he/she is upset.

17. "I would like to say how I think I just contributed to our upset."

18. "May we take a 30-minute break and then talk again? I will listen first."

19. "I am upset right now, but it isn't your fault."

20. "What can I do that would make you feel better?"

Larger Repairs

Too many self-help books leave couples with the message that, "If you read this book and follow every instruction, you will have a blissful marriage." In our experience, many couples have entrenched patterns of negativity that will crop up in the middle of trying to do a "helpful" exercise. Sometimes we can get ourselves into shape; sometimes we need a personal trainer who knows where to start and how to help push us through the difficult exercises. With a 50% divorce rate, it seems to us that most couples could use some type of help learning to repair the ruptures in their relationship before it is too late. Nothing makes us sadder in our coaching-counseling practices than having couples arrive thinking their relationship is over and nothing can help. There are so many good, sound tools that can help couples from all walks of life. Let's look at the ingredients of effective help, a few types of relationship help, and who may benefit from each.

The Ingredients of Effective Help

In addition to attending a workshop or seminar, couples often need a course of individual help. Regardless of what's going on in your marriage or the degree of relationship distress, three ingredients constitute effective help: education, tools, and structure. You will want to make certain that the counselor or coach you chose could help you in each of these areas.

Education: All couples have a learning curve if they want to have a rock solid relationship. Because education offers a model of what can be expected over the course of a long relationship, it accelerates the learning curve. Understanding what is "normal" also helps you both to stop worrying about the challenges you face. In addition, relationship education courses teach you how your childhood history plays a significant part in your marriage struggles; knowing each other's history leads to more understanding of the reactions, needs, and limitations you each bring to the relationship. Learning what you each need and how to meet those needs brings safety and security to your relationship. And safety and security are the *foundation* of your relationship "house."

Tools: To achieve a rock solid relationship, all couples need tools and both partners working together on the relationship. Think about it this way: Houses aren't built just because we fall in love with them. Maybe we envision them, but to erect them takes carpentry tools and lots of team effort.

The same is true for relationships. We each need communication "tools" that bring about safe conversation; these tools comprise listening skills, respectful talking skills, and the willingness and ability to initiate a serious conversation. (Yes, you can have these tools!) Another important relationship "tool" is the ability to manage mounting upset, to stay available and present, and to attune to your partner in the face of irritation. (Yes, you can learn to do this!) Yet other tools such as memory, awareness, and self-motivation can be used to actively demonstrate you care for your partner through loving actions. (Yes, these tools are available to you through education and by learning your partner's love languages!) And all the above skills and tools will be called upon when you need to repair a conflict. In case you need to have it spelled out: Relationship tools can be learned—and with practice comes mastery.

If education is the foundation and tools are what we use to build the house, then structure is the "framing" needed to build the walls and a roof. Without it, there is no house!

In general, structure is the ingredient that creates the shape and form of your relationship. It includes the firewall boundaries that protect your relationship, providing the safety needed for your relationship to grow (and heal). Structure in communication involves a system you learn or establish that helps you to take turns talking, make certain you really heard one another, and to validate your partner's point of view before you chime in with your own. It also includes how you communicate using the Intentional Dialogue process or the steps you use to repair a disconnection or conflict as in a "do-over." Many of us balk at the thought of using structure as too confining and contrived, but changing bad habits and reactions requires the kind of structure that will facilitate change. Without it, the roof will fall in.

Relationship counseling requires the use of all three of these ingredients in collaboration with each other to build a rock solid relationship. The insight that comes from educating yourself about your relationship needs and issues will not create change unless you know what to do with it. Without knowledge and structure, tools get dropped when conflict or disconnection occurs. And structure becomes rigid and boring without the other two ingredients to bring your relationship to fulfillment. These three ingredients—education, tools, and structure—together can transform a house of cards into a mansion of love that we call a rock solid relationship.

When you reach out for help to a coach or counselor, make sure you ask a few questions about style, training, and credentials. Make certain who you chose incorporates all the necessary ingredients for the best possible outcome.

Types of Relationship Help

Education and Enrichment—A Major Deposit in the Relationship Savings Account: One of the biggest deposits you can make into your relationship savings account is that of putting the time and energy into learning new tools, gaining fresh insights, and experimenting with new relationship enhancing exercises. Many studies have shown that relationship education brings the most lasting positive changes. This is because we all need to learn some of the basics of what is normal in a relationship and what tools could help us when we run into trouble. Good relationship education also inspires and reignites romance and adventure.

While teaching the powerful *Getting the Love You Want* workshop for couples, we have met a number of couples who attend one relationship retreat a year. They find an interesting workshop offering from an on-line search and then pick a nice destination to make the experience a real retreat away from their lives. They refresh their bond, learn new tools, and have some meaningful "light-bulb" moments. It isn't that their marriage is in trouble; by attending the workshops, they hope to avert trouble by staying connected and putting their relationship first.

Not all couples can afford a retreat each year, but with effort most couples can set aside an evening, a day, or a weekend to put undivided time into their relationship while learning a few new tricks. They can read a self-help book (start with this one) or listen to an educational podcast together. For example, many of our clients "retreat" from their daily demands and take a day or weekend to practice the exercises from such books as *Rock Solid Relationships, Love Languages, Hot Monogamy* and *Getting the Sex You Want.* Needless to say, their efforts go a long way toward funding their relationship savings accounts!

Also, there is a wealth of free information online. Take turns finding YouTube videos, TED talks, or other resources dealing with couples' enrichment and information. Set a day aside to watch a series of videos and talks about what you are learning. There are videos hosted by Harville Hendrix, John Gottman, Ester Perel, Pat Love, and many more brilliant and entertaining relationship experts. Set a goal to fill up your relationship savings account with these major investments that will give you something tangible to reach for when you need a tool.

Make it a habit to grow your knowledge base and try something new. Thanks to research and science, we really do know how to create and maintain lasting love—and the information and tools can be yours for the asking. We think that all—yes, all—couples benefit greatly from relationship education. Whether it is a newly engaged couple or a pair who has been battling for years, couples always grow from immersion learning. However, many couples need to continue beyond the workshop or class with a coach or counselor who can offer more guidance.

Relationship Coaching: Coaching with couples is done from the privacy of your home over the telephone. Relationship coaches, like any life coach, help you to set your goals for an ideal relationship and work through the obstacles. Coaches usually ask for a once per week, six-month commitment. Their job is to help inspire, motivate, problem solve, and brainstorm your way to success. Coaches use assessment tools, exercises, and communication techniques that both educate and train. Coaching can be done privately, or in a group. Group coaching is more cost effective and has the benefit of learning from the experiences of other couples.

These sessions are usually offered as anonymous webinar and conference call groups and/or as private telephone sessions. Coaches are often well-trained couple counselors who focus on outcomes versus deep process. The couples that benefit most from coaching are ones who are both committed to staying together and who aren't currently involved in heated fights.

Counseling Sessions: Couples with major avoidance behaviors—those who are working through an affair or other breech of trust, those considering divorce, or ones who have been "stuck" in negative patterns for years—would likely need counseling. Also, if either of you struggles with depression, anxiety, addictions, or uncontrollable anger, a counselor is best suited to help you with these types of issues. Sessions as a couple with a counselor are more expensive than coaching, but if you feel you need the privacy and focus such a session gives, this is the path for you. (Many couple counselors can bill insurance.) Plan for working with a trained marriage counselor for about 12 sessions spread over four to six months.

Get Help Fast and Get On With the Fun

Your intimate relationship is a big investment. Do all you can on your own to enrich and maintain that investment. When you reach your own, normal human limitations, act quickly to get the help you need. Although the faster you act, the less help necessary, it is never too late to reverse the damage and return to the loving, fun, relaxing, and joyful bond you once enjoyed.

The benefits of regular maintenance and repairs cannot be overstated. All of us stop in our tracks when a beautifully maintained vintage automobile drives down the street. Those solid old cars with shiny paint, rolled leather upholstery, and maybe even with the top down make us all sigh and think, "What treasures! Someone maintained the cars impeccably over the years, or worked hard to restore them to their glory." That is exactly what it feels like to live in a marriage that has been maintained or at some point has been rescued from rust and ruin in order to restore its glory. It feels like a treasure. It is a marriage that makes others stop and stare and think about how lucky that couple is, to have such a gem of a relationship. In Bonnie's Raitt's words, "Let's give 'em somethin' to talk about."

Reflections

Read over the "20 Possible Repair Attempts" and think about which ones you have used in the past and found successful. Ask your partner to discuss the list and decide together what would be helpful. Put the list on the refrigerator next to the emergency numbers!

Think of a time when you felt too upset to make a repair. Write about what you think might have been going on for you then. Stubbornness? Inflexibility or needing to be right? Write about what might go on in your mind that is an obstacle to offering or accepting a repair. Now write about what your partner may be thinking and feeling that affects his or her ability to offer or receive a repair overture.

Write about the current issues in your relationship that need some repair. List the regular upsets, frustrations, and grievances. Which repair is indicated for each one? Which are do-it-yourself and which, if any, are issues for a workshop, coach, or counselor?

Conclusion

"Your life will not go unnoticed,
because I will notice it.
Your life will not go unwitnessed,
because I will be your witness."

—From the movie, Shall We Dance?

Nothing is more compelling to humans than to love another and be loved in return. And nothing is more devastating than to stand in the smoking ruins of a once-loving relationship and wonder what happened. Understanding where you are and what you are feeling, we have created this road map of a book to offer you a beacon of hope and to set you on a course to recovering your connection and making your love last.

Have the courage and faith to commence the journey! And know you are not alone along the road. Every couple that attends a workshop such as *Getting the Love You Want* in order to fix their marriage discovers that they are not alone in their struggles. They move from feeling isolated in despair to realizing that marriage is hard work for us all. We don't need to hide our mistakes, rather we can learn from other's victories. Coaches and counselors have walked thousands of other couples through the dark days of relationship troubles and have witnessed their emergence from the tunnel of despair into a renewed life, into a rock solid relationship.

No one is guaranteed a marriage without hurt, disappointment, un-pleasantness, or sheer awfulness. People stumble and sometimes fall flat on their faces for ridiculous reasons. Babies are born to us with health problems. Partners become ill, lose jobs, and bring difficult extended families into the marriage. But what separates couples who get up, dust themselves off, take the hand of their partner, and find joy in the new day are those who can replenish their relationship accounts. These resilient couples can withstand the challenges of time because they know the keys to making relationship deposits when their accounts have been depleted.

Needing some help to learn the keys to making those deposits is nothing of which to be ashamed nor embarrassed. No matter how much or little our parents showed us about a good marriage, none of us were handed a relationship "toolbox" in childhood. Plus, intimate relationships demand the most complicated set of interactions that humans encounter. Under the tremendous stress of relationship conflict, the pull of negativity is as strong as the pull of gravity. And the longer you have succumbed to negativity, the more you will need education or coaching to be the booster rocket that pulls your relationship free of the gravitational pull of negativity and put it back into orbit. Once in orbit, maintenance and regular repairs will keep it there.

The work of pulling away from negativity is extremely challenging, but the rewards are immeasurable. We mentioned earlier in the book some sociological and psychological benefits of a rock solid relationship, but they bear repeating here:

1. Statistics show that married people live longer than their unmarried counterparts and have higher happiness levels (CBS News Cleveland, 2014; Miller, Hollist *et al*, 2013; Parker-Pope, 2010). Long-married couples know how to take care of each another, know what is normal and what is unusual in their partner's routine, and have the ability to weather a crisis together.

2. As the opening quote of this chapter states, being in a solid relationship with someone who knows you *deeply* is validating, an acknowledgement that who you are and what you do is not going unnoticed. To bear witness to someone's life is to give that person significance. We are one among billions, and what sets us apart is that someone cares if we are sick or well, happy or sad, fulfilled or floundering.

3. People in long-term relationships make more money, have more creative outlets, and meet more of their personal goals (Waite, 2001; Hirschl, Atobelli and Rank, 2003). This is likely due to having someone who has known them for a long time to encourage them over their hurdles.

4. Children with parents in a committed, in-it-for-the-long haul relationship do better at school, make more money as adults, have higher self-esteem, and report more optimism and less depression and anxiety (Kim, 2011; Wallerstein, Lewis and Blakeslee, 2001). They also have a better chance at lasting love if they see it between their parents.

5. Adult children with non-divorced parents feel closer to their parents than their peers with divorced parents, because divorce weakens the bonds between parents and children over the long run. That is, adult children of divorce describe the relationships with both their mother and their father less positively than adults whose parents stayed married, possibly because time with the children is spread between both parents and, therefore, is less frequent when there has been a divorce. The same goes for grandchildren (Taylor, 2012; Amato and Afifi, 2006; King, 2003; and Amato and Sobolewski, 2001).

6. Divorce is very expensive—financially and emotionally. Most divorced individuals have far less financial resources once those resources have been divided in half, and getting back on a sound financial footing can take each partner many years (Avellar and Smock, 2005). Even if money isn't a worry, the emotional cost of divorce is almost always huge. Whatever your status and experience in the aftermath of divorce, the fact of failing at what you once were certain would last a lifetime often presents one with an abiding sense of loss and regret.

7. Long-term partners have more active sex lives than their single cohort (Heiman, Long *et al*, 2011). As we age, having sex with someone with whom we are familiar is a lot easier than starting up with a new person and an old body.

8. Long-term lasting relationships are good for mental health. Married men and women are less depressed and less anxious (Musick and Bumpass, 2012). Older couples have built-in companions, best friends, and helpmates and struggle less with isolation and the difficulties of spending too much time alone.

9. When elderly Americans are asked about the proudest accomplishment of their long lives, they usually refer to their marriage. Then they are proud of their kids and/or their careers.

10. If you stay and work on things, you have a chance to grow into the magnificent human being you were born to become. Running away from your current relationship will only result in your bringing 50% of the problems with you. If your bad behavior, lazy habits regarding marriage, poor boundaries, bad communication skills, lack of prioritizing love, and immaturity contributed to the problems in your relationship, then ending your relationship and hoping for a new one that will withstand the same issues is taking a big and unnecessary risk. Staying and trying to work on your current relationship has more of a chance of success!

Despite your challenges today, you and your partner CAN have a rock solid relationship that stands the test of time! Our Seven Keys can be the stepping-stones to a relationship that will make you thrilled to wake up with your partner by your side every day for the rest of your life.

To make remembering the keys easier, we leave you with this summary of the Seven Keys to restore your connection and make your love last. Perhaps you'll want to copy the list, tuck it in a place you frequent (your purse or wallet, for example), and refer to it often. Like Benjamin Franklin who created a system of working monthly throughout his life on one of 13 virtues, you and your partner might consider working monthly on a particular relationship key and keeping it up throughout the year, rotating the keys until all the keys become second nature and your relationship savings account is overflowing.

Seven Keys to Restore Your Connection and Make Your Love Last

Key #1: Return Your Partner to Priority Status: Nothing is as important as your relationship. Think of it as your retirement account! Sex alone isn't enough to keep your marriage strong, children aren't enough to ensure your marriage lasts, and all the money in the world can't buy you love. But your relationship will sustain you long after the kids have left, your body sags, and your career is over! It's connection and closeness that will fill your days with joy and keep your marriage rock solid. That connection and closeness comes from putting time and energy into your partner each day, every day, for all of your life.

Key #2: Love is a Verb, So Focus on the Action: You can't just say, "I love you" and leave it at that. Love requires thousands of actions spread over time. Show tenderness and affection daily, affirm your partner's actions, be generous with appreciations, and encourage him or her when he or she feels doubtful, down, or demoralized. Be responsible; when you take on a task, follow through. Be giving of your time and talents. When a holiday, birthday, or anniversary arrives, celebrate it; put time into choosing a gift and ask for ideas if needed. Make ample time for you and your partner to be alone and enjoy each other's company. Keep romance and adventure alive. Go on dates, have a weekend alone, go out with friends, and have fun.

Key #3: Negativity Kills Love, So Cut It Out! Watch for the ways in which negativity slides into your style of relating. Put energy every day into thinking positively about your partner. Stop all your shaming, blaming, criticizing, stonewalling, displays of contempt, defensiveness, interrupting, and avoiding. Do your part, don't be negative about your partner's part, and revel in the results.

Key #4: Communication is Key, So Dial Up the Dialogue: Good communication is the means of turning conflict into connection. No one arrived at committed relationships with a real knack for communication. Learning good communication skills takes work and an understanding that the stakes are higher and the triggers are quicker at home; our childhood wounds make us more vulnerable with our partners. As you come to know more about your feelings and needs, you can express them to your partner. You also can learn new tools to assure that you speak in a way your partner can hear, and listen to your partner in a way he or she feels safe to speak.

Key #5: Build a Firewall to Protect Your Relationship: Your couple-dom constantly is being bombarded with countless distractions, strains, pulls, and demands. Healthy boundaries with children, coworkers, family, friends, and even pets will help to actualize Key #1, making your relationship the priority in your life. Boundaries of confidentiality ensure that you always turn *first* to your partner with your news, upsets, fears, and concerns. In this way, you protect your marriage's sanctity and your partner's feelings. Firewalls keep friends and coworkers in their place and safeguard you from having emotional or physical affairs.

Key #6: Keep Your Sex Life Alive: Sex is the glue that keeps us close. Lasting relationships benefit from remaining physical. Practicing good intimate habits and turning around your poor intimacy habits will improve things not only in the bedroom but also in every room in your relationship house. For most couples, sexual connection—a major means of reassurance, stress relief, and showing love—makes for significant credits in the relationship savings account. It is what sets our intimate relationship apart from any and every other connection in our life.

Key #7: Make a Practice of Regular Maintenance and Repair: Because all intimate relationships face challenges, big and small, you need to know how to maintain the relationship harmony and, when you find the relationship flailing, to restore the harmony with repairs. Most of the time the needed repair will be "do it yourselves," but some ruptures will require learning new insights, gaining new tools, or getting guidance through the rockiest parts. It's challenging to keep a relationship in tiptop shape! Marriage is work. Work at it everyday. Cherish it every day. Make it last.

Our Seven Keys to restoring connection and making love last give you a plan to establish a relationship savings account and regularly make deposits. The miracle of compound interest gives you exponential growth from your investments. Take up the challenge and get started today on creating a rock solid relationship. You CAN restore your connection and make your love last a lifetime!

Chapter References (in order of appearance)

Key #1: Return Your Partner to Priority Status

Wallerstein, Judith and Lewis, Julia. "The Unexpected Legacy of Divorce: Report of a 25 Year Study." Psychoanalytic Psychology. 2004. Vol. 21(3), 353–370.

Emery, Robert. *The Truth About Children and Divorce.* NY: Plume, 2006.

Root, Andrew. *The Children of Divorce: The Loss of Family as the Loss of Being.* Ada, MI: Baker Publishing, 2010.

Eaker Weil, Bonnie. *Make Up, Don't Break Up: Finding and Keeping Love for Singles and Couples.* Avon, MA: Adams Media, 2010.

Harvard Health Publications. "Marriage and Men's Health." July 1, 2010.

Parker-Pope, Tara. "Is Marriage Good for Your Health?" *The New York Times Magazine,* April 14, 2010.

Proulx, Christine and Snyder-Rivas, Linley. "The Longitudinal Associations between Marital Happiness, Problems, and Self-Rated Health." *Journal of Family Psychology*, Apr. 2013. Vol. 27(2), 194-202. Study highlights in an article in the University of Missouri News by Kate McIntyre entitled, "Happily Married Couples Consider Themselves Healthier, Says MU Expert."

Key #2: Love is a Verb, So Focus on the Action

Forsell, Lena M. and Åström, Jan A. "Meanings of Hugging: From Greeting Behavior to Touching Implications." *Comprehensive Psychology.* 2012. Vol. 1(1). Study highlights in an article on PassionSante.be website entitled, "Hugs, But It Feels Good."

Dobson, Roger. "Embrace Hugging: Daily Cuddles Can Combat Infections and Lowers Risk of Heart Disease." *Daily Mail.* Nov. 10, 2012.

Dillner, Luisa. Love by Numbers: *The Hidden Facts Behind Everyone's Relationships.* London: Profile Books, 2004.

O'Connor, Dagmar. *How to Make Love to the Same Person for the Rest of Your Life and Still Love It.* 2nd ed. London: Virgin Black Lace, 2005.

Northrup, C., Schwartz, P., and Witte, James. *The Normal Bar: The Surprising Secrets of Happy Couples and What They Reveal About Creating a New Normal in Your Relationship.* NY: Harmony Books, 2014.

Foster, Brooke Lea. "Will Your Marriage Last? What Social Scientists Have Learned from Putting Couples Under the Microscope." *Washingtonian.* Dec. 18, 2012. Highlights findings of the National Marriage Project, University of Virginia.

Society for Personality and Social Psychology. "Keep Romance Alive with Double Dates." *Science Daily.* Feb. 10, 2014.

Frederickson, Barbara. *Love 2.0: Creating Happiness and Health in Moments of Connection.* Rev. ed. NY: Plume, 2013.

Key #3: Negativity Kills Love, So Cut It Out!

Gottman, John and Silver, Nan. *The Seven Principles for Making Marriage Work.* Rev. ed. NY: Harmony Books, 2015.

Hendrix, Harville. *Getting the Love You Want: A Guide for Couples.* Rev. ed. NY: Henry Holt & Co., 2007.

Hanson, Rick and Mendius, Richard. *The Practical Neuroscience of Buddha's Brain: Happiness, Love & Wisdom.* Oakland, CA: New Harbinger Publications, 2009.

University of California Los Angeles Laboratory of Neuro Imaging. "Brain Trivia." 2008.

Key #4: Communication Is Key, So Dial Up the Dialogue

Gottman, John and Silver, Nan. *The Seven Principles for Making Marriage Work.* Rev. ed. NY: Harmony Books, 2015.

Northrup, C., Schwartz, P. and Witte, James. *The Normal Bar: The Surprising Secrets of Happy Couples and What They Reveal About Creating a New*

Normal in Your Relationship. NY: Harmony Books, 2014.

Larsen, Earnie. *Stage II Recovery: Life Beyond Addiction.* NY: Harper One, 2009.

Hendrix, Harville. *Getting the Love You Want: A Guide for Couples.* Rev. ed. NY: Henry Holt & Co., 2007.

Key #5: Build a Firewall to Protect Your Relationship

National Opinion Research Center. General Social Survey, 2010.

Glass, Shirley. *Not "Just Friends": Rebuilding Your Trust and Recovering Your Sanity After Infidelity,* NY: Atria, 2004.

Schulte, Brigid. "'Til Death Do Us Part? No Way. Gray Divorce on the Rise." *The Washington Post.* Oct. 8, 2014. Article cites research of S.L. Brown and I.F. Lin, Bowling Green State University.

Key #6: Keep Your Sex Life Alive

Scheele, E., Wille, A., Kendrick, K.M., Stoffel-Wagner, B., Becker, B., Gunturkun, O., Maier, W., and Hurlemann, R. "Oxytocin enhances brain reward system responses in men viewing the face of their female partner." *Proceedings of the National Academy of Sciences,* 2013; DOI:

Gray, John. *Men Are from Mars, Women Are from Venus.* NY: Harper, 2012.

University College London, Research Dept. of Infection and Population Health. "Changes in Sexual Attitudes and Lifestyles in Britain Through the Life Course and Over Time: Findings from the National Surveys of Sexual Attitudes and Lifestyles." *The Lancet.* Nov., 2013.

Medical Center for Female Sexuality (MCFS). "Female Orgasm." MCFS Web site accessed March 23, 2015.

Berman, Laura. "The Top Ten Female Climax Myths That Men Still Believe." Jan. 22, 2013. Everyday Health Web site accessed March 23, 2015.

Barbach, Lonnie. *For Yourself: The Fulfillment of Female Sexuality.* NY: Signet, 2000.

Kerner, Ian. "Do Women Like Porn As Much as Men?" Web blog post. **The Chart. CNN, April 28, 2011. Accessed March 23, 2015.**

Conclusion

CBS News Cleveland. "Study: Married Couples Live Longer, Healthier Lives Than Singles." Nov. 14, 2014. A news report highlighting the research of Hui Liu of Michigan State University and Corinne Reczek at the University of Cincinnati.

Miller, R.B., Hollist, C.S., Olsen, J., and Law, D. "Marital Quality and Health Over Years: A Growth Curve Analysis." *Journal of Marriage and Family.* May 20, 2013.

Parker-Pope, Tara. "Is Marriage Good for Your Health?" *The New York Times Magazine,* April 14, 2010.

Waite, Linda. *The Case for Marriage: Why Married People are Happier, Healthier and Better Off Financially.* NY: Broadway Books, 2001.

Hirschl, T.A., Altobelli, J., and Rank, M.R. "Does Marriage Increase the Odds of Affluence? Exploring the Life Course Probabilities." *Journal of Marriage and Family.* Nov. 2003. Vol. 65(4), 927–938.

Kim, H.S. "Consequences of Parental Divorce for Child Development." *American Sociological Review.* June, 2011. Vol. 76(3), 487-511.

Wallerstein, J., Lewis, J.M., and Blakeslee, S. *The Unexpected Legacy of Divorce: A 25 Year Landmark Study.* NY: Hachette Books, 2001.

Taylor, Chris. "Double the Trouble When Divorced Parents Get Old." *Chicago Tribune.* Oct.19, 2012.

Amato, Paul R. and Afifi, Tamara D. "Feeling Caught Between Parents: Adult Children's Relations with Parents and Subjective Well-Being." *Journal of Marriage and Family.* 2006. Vol. 68(1), 231.

King, Valarie. "The Legacy of a Grandparent's Divorce: Consequences for Ties Between Grandparents and Grandchildren." *Journal of Marriage and Family.* 2003. Vol. 65, 179.

Amato, Paul R. and Sobolewski, Juliana M. "The Effects of Divorce and Marital Discord on Adult Children's Psychological Well-Being." *American Sociological Review.* 2001. Vol. 66, 917.

Avellar, Sarah, and Smock, Pamela J. "The Economic Consequences of the Dissolution of Cohabiting Unions." *Journal of Marriage and Family.* May 2005. Vol. 67(2), 315–327.

Heiman, J.R., Long, S.J., Smith, S.N., Fisher, W.A., and Sand, M.S. "Sexual satisfaction and relationship happiness in midlife and older couples in five countries." *Archives of Sexual Behavior.* 2011. Vol. 40, 741-753.

Musick, Kelly, and Bumpass, Larry. "Reexamining the Case for Marriage: Union Formation and Changes in Well-being." *Journal of Marriage and Family.* Feb. 2012. Vol. 74(1), 1-18.

Meet the Authors

 **Norene Gonsiewski**, MSW, LCSW, has worked with couples and individuals since 1980. As a relationship coach, counselor and educator she has taught thousands of individuals how to build lasting and passionate relationships. In 1997, with Tim Higdon, Norene founded Portland Relationship Center through which she and Tim practice Imago Relationship Therapy and offer resources for creating healthy and lasting relationships. Norene is a dynamic teacher of workshops for couples and individuals.

Norene is affectionately known at the "Relationship Guru." As such, she is a sought-after guest on television talk shows. In addition to co-authoring *Rock Solid Relationship: Seven Keys to Restore Your Connection*

and Make Your Love Last, Norene also is the co-author with Nicole Jon Sievers, of *It's Your Mind: Own It! A Manual for Every Teen.* Norene believes that healthy relationships form the heart of a community.

Norene lives in Portland, Oregon, with her best friend and husband of 35 years, Tom. She and Tom raised two wonderful children.

 **Timothy Higdon**, MS, LPC, has been working to help people build strong relationships throughout his 35-year career as a therapist and counselor. And he is even more passionate today about his mission—guiding couples safely through relationship obstacles to the lasting change and deep connection for which they yearn.

Currently, Tim is co-owner of 3Rivers Center for Relationship in Bend, OR and Portland Relationship Center. He has been a treatment and executive director of a residential treatment center and was instrumental in founding several youth and family programs.

At the core of Tim's work is Imago Relationship Therapy (IRT). Over the years, he has helped hundreds of couples and individuals using IRT tools. As an Imago Workshop Presenter for individuals and couples and a Certified Imago Consultant for professionals and educators, Tim is engaging and enthusiastic. His style is down-to-earth, practical, and approachable.

Using the tools he teaches, Tim has been happily married to his wife, Susan, for 32 years. Together they have raised two children to adulthood. Music feeds his soul, and he still finds time to fly fish for steelhead and trout in the Northwest's most beautiful rivers.

Made in the USA
San Bernardino, CA
24 September 2015